THINK/WRITE
A Guide to Research Writing
Across the Curriculum

Linda K. Shamoon
University of Rhode Island

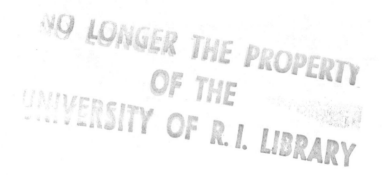

Kendall/Hunt
Publishing Company
Dubuque, Iowa

B   403835   01

CONTENTS

INTRODUCTION

What is your response when an instructor announces that a "research paper" is a requirement for a course? Do you immediately envision hours spent in a library and late nights spent pecking at the typewriter? Do you wonder how long the paper must be and how you will get through the extra reading? Do you worry about figuring out just what sort of paper the instructor has in mind by the term "research" paper.

This text is devoted to exploring research papers. It will help you to find out just what instructors may have in mind when they say "research," and let you try your hand at a variety of research papers. Its aim is to turn your image of research from an activity centered in the library to one of action and intellectual challenge across the campus by introducing you to some of the research activities and problems of professionals in major academic areas. It lays out methodology for you to follow as you set about research projects of your own, and offers particular help with the writing of the paper. Wherever possible this text starts with your experience and draws on campus resources to enlarge your concepts of research papers and your opportunities to practice.

Before we jump into your elaborate project, however, we need to review some shared experiences in writing, to build up a vocabulary between us that will help us communicate about writing, and we need to practice a few important skills that will make success come a little easier as you try the various research papers in this text. These are the concerns of the Preview sections. The five Preview sections will review many of the steps of writing a term paper, and will ask you to do many short writing projects which, when brought together, will result in a short term paper. I hope you will use these Preview sections as opportunities to review what you know about writing and to explore new ideas about writing and research.

Preview - Part I
The Writing Process

In writing this text I have assumed that each of you has had some experience with term papers and a good deal of experience writing essays for teachers. It is these experiences I would like to draw upon at the beginning. Each of us, no doubt, has heard good advice from these instructors about writing, such as: find a subject and narrow it down, make a thesis statement, write an outline, write a first draft, rewrite, and proofread. If a term paper is the assignment, then a few more steps are thrown into the mix, such as outside reading, note taking, and footnoting, but the basic process remains the same.

This is all good advice; for some students it is very helpful advice. But researchers of composition have found there are some problems with this advice. They found that many good writers simply skip or cut short some of these "necessary" steps. Many good writers, for example, do not make outlines and yet their papers are organized. In addition, these researchers found that some steps sometimes inhibit the starting up and the flow of writing, such as the dictum of writing a thesis sentence before an exploratory, first draft. ("How can I know what I want to write before I actually write it?" ask some writers.) Finally, these researchers have found that for many students rewriting and proofreading are the same activities, but for professional writers these are usually dramatically different tasks.

1

For these and many other reasons some writing teachers have turned to offering guidelines that more closely resemble the process that successful writers use as they write. They suggest that professional writers engage in the following activities: perception, or getting to know your subject matter close up and from several perspectives; visualizing the audience, or judging who is listening and what they need to hear; writing a first draft, or getting it down on paper and creating order; rewriting, or tinkering with words, sentences and paragraphs to make the writing shine; editing, or getting the details of spelling and grammar correct. Notice that in these guidelines, some traditional elements are not featured (such as outlining) and some are added (such as audience analysis). It is my experience that if these activities are imitated, writing tends to be a more active, real world and immediate experience than the formal and formula-like chores of the more traditional approach.

Other researchers of composition have rendered these activities even more accessible through their observations that the writing process is recursive rather than step-like. That is, they found that professional writers move back and forth through the tasks of writing as they go along, perceiving their subject and also writing down interesting phrases and passages, or rewriting a passage for tighter language while continuing to perceive the subject, and so on. Furthermore they have found that writers tend to move through the process in their own particular ways. This knowledge should be liberating to most of us, because within the limits of sensible guidelines we, each, can develop our own process in the order that leads to the most success.

Unwritten, but very much present behind process-oriented writing activities, is the need for us to make ourselves aware of what it is we are doing as we write our essays, as we struggle over starting and rushing through drafts. We need to find a way to capture and look at our own process, compare it to the guidelines and then change those aspects of our writing process which might improve by doing them differently.

The way to put all of this advice to use is simply to start writing--two kinds of writing. One is to start writing an essay on a subject that might well evolve into a term paper, and the other is to start writing in a journal about the writing. Both kinds of writing will help us to understand what is happening when we try to wrestle our subject matter onto the written page.

To help you get the essay started, let us adapt the activities listed above to our purposes. First, choose a subject of interest to you. Get involved with your subject as you begin to write about it. Take time to remember it carefully, close-up, sensually, using your own, honest perceptions, and remembering what others had to say, gathering in your thoughts, and exploring your insights. Using this level of involvement as a standard, write about a subject--a person, an event, a concept, idea, theory, or academic study--with which you may have been fascinated (or at least curious) at some time during the past few semesters. Perhaps you have already written a paper on this subject or are an expert by way of a hobby or a job. Whatever the source of familiarity, write an essay about something *within* that subject that you know well, that you think is important, and would like to get to know in more detail.

Use this first essay to remember what you know about the subject, to focus in on some particularly interesting issues or aspects of the subject, and even to explain why the subject is significant or important to you personally. Do not be afraid to be passionate or personal in this draft; use this draft as a means of becoming involved. Develop a draft that represents the best writing you can muster at this time.

Turning to the second type of writing, the writer's journal, make an entry which lays out your personal writing process and compares it to that suggested by this Preview section. Be honest in reviewing the steps that you usually take when writing, and add your opinion of the steps reviewed here. Finally, include your thoughts about the first attempts at the first essay. Try to describe how you started, what guided your writing, and what you think of the quality of the writing you did for this first step.

Preview - Part II
Audience; Adding 2 Sources

Since one goal of the first assignment is to get you involved with your subject, your essay should spark your personal interest, but may not be a first class piece of writing that you would be proud to share with a peer or to show to an instructor. This is as it should be, for we have only begun to explore the writing process and tie it into research writing.

One way to bring this paper forward to a tight, focused, well written essay is to review it with an eye toward a particular audience. Many students claim that they are writing for a general audience, but you will make much more effective writing decisions if you give an identity to your audience. For example, suppose the audience for your essay turns out to be fourth and fifth graders. Would not that effect the content of your essay? Would you now use different words, simpler sentences, and try for a different tone? Would not the age of this audience effect every aspect of your writing? Or suppose your audience was a gathering of powerful politicians who have gathered to learn from you, an expert, about the subject. Would you not have a different point to make, using different words, to create a very different tone? Finding the identity of our audience usually forces us to make very specific decisions about all the elements of writing. (For an in depth look at this subject, see Chapter VIII.)

Let us specify an audience identity for the next draft of your essay. Let us agree that your audience will be your classmates. They are your age, well educated, articulate, and struggling through a similar assignment. They are, therefore, a somewhat familiar group, sharing a world of experiences, vocabulary and values upon which you may draw and depend as you write. They are also probably fairly sympathetic to you as a writer, but let us also assume that they are not very familiar with your subject. You stand before them as the expert.

What does this mean for your next draft of your essay? Consider content first. You must decide what are the one or two major points this audience should remember after they have read your paper. In order for them to understand these points, what information must you provide? How much background? How much history? How much technical detail? How much description or discussion? Do they already know the importance of your subject or will you have to explain the significance? Must you tie the subject to their lives, or will they be able to see the connections themselves? If you are an expert, will you explain the source of your expertise or knowledge?

Next consider related aspects of style. What would be the right language and tone for this audience? Should you be as formal as possible, or would you relate better using occasional slang? What will be your opening strategy to "hook" them into the rest of the paper, and how will you sound a note of finality and emphasis at the end so they will remember the paper? What language and sentencing will you avoid so that you will not lose this audience midway through the paper?

In order to contemplate some of the answers to these questions, use our journal to try out a few sentences and paper plans or outlines to test your approach to your audience. Share this with your instructor and classmates.

3

Another way I would like to add depth to your paper is to bring in two or three outside sources. Since you have chosen a subject that you know in some depth already, you may not yet feel the need to introduce outside sources, but at the very least these sources may be used to add authority to your own writing and discussion. In addition, there are surely some aspects of your subject about which you would like to know more or have more information with which to support your interpretation. Of course, touching base with a few, well chosen outside sources might help you focus your essay even further, helping you to select the more important points and decide what may be omitted.

I am well aware that introducing outside sources may add some complicated tasks to writing this draft, tasks such as using the library and getting bogged down in reading, so let us set some realistic limitations. Firstly, limit yourself to two easily accessible sources which offer highly focused discussions of your subject. I suggest the following as likely sources: an article from an encyclopedia recommended by your reference librarian; a textbook in which your subject is only a part or which divides your subject into several parts; notes from class lectures; or an extensive article from a magazine which you might easily locate. Even though this search might take you to the library, try not to get bogged down in endless shelf hunting for a book; encyclopedias and introductory books are usually readily available and easy to locate. (Even though later exercises in the text will make you familiar with the reference area of the library and with many, many research books, I do assume you know how to use the card catalogue and how to locate a book in the library. If this is not the case for you, take time to familiarize yourself with these two areas.)

Secondly, make sure your sources are portable in some way so that you may bring them to class. If you are dealing with library materials, either make sure you may check out the books or that you may copy the originals within reasonable time and expense.

Thirdly, do not do a thorough, in depth reading of the two sources just yet; instead, browse through them, making sure that the sources seem to touch upon the sort of information you might need to add to your paper, and that they are written in only slightly more technical depth and language than you, yourself, are used to reading about on this subject. Once you feel comfortable with the potential of your two sources, turn your attention to your essay and your journal. On one side of a journal page make a list of the contents of your paper, perhaps paragraph by paragraph or point by point. On the other side of the page, make a list of the information apparently provided by the two sources that you might be able to use in the next draft of your paper. Your task here is not to list every detail of the outside source, but to surmise what information the sources are likely to provide that will enrich your own essay. Outside sources might help your essay by providing: 1) factual information and details you might not know; 2) opinions of authorities that will back up your statements; and 3) a manner of dealing with the subject that aids your own focus or organization. Outside sources can sometimes add too much information with too much authority, forcing us to lose sight of our own views or writing aims. If, however, we start by inventorying our own insights and selecting information from the sources, we will find our writing enriched rather than swamped by outside sources.

Using your audience analysis, you should write another draft of the essay, and note within the text where you intend to refer to outside sources.

As soon as using outside sources becomes part of the writing project, students often worry about using footnotes, when to use quotation marks, and how to refer to the ideas of others without plagiarizing. I would like to suggest that these concerns have easy answers and that the real problem for writers is to select and integrate the outside materials so as to give room for their own ideas and words rather than to obscure them. We can easily answer your questions about footnoting and making reference to outside sources by following a few exercises, but we must also learn how to select and use these sources to set us free to write our own essay.

In order for you to feel more comfortable with referencing and documentation, our exercises begin with footnoting, then take a look at the problem of referencing within the text. The next Preview section will continue this study by reviewing some other choices you have as a writer when dealing with outside sources.

Unlike other research writing textbooks, this text does not lay out one system of documentation for you to memorize. Since many academic fields have their own systems of documentation, it is much more important for you to be able to adapt quickly to any system by recognizing the key features of all footnotes and bibliographies. This is surely a better approach than memorizing a new system for each course. We will further cut down the task by concentrating now on footnote formats, and study bibliography in depth in a later chapter.

As a first step it is necessary for you to appreciate why footnoting must be rigidly standardized, and yet why it is still evolving in many fields. I am sure that you are aware that the purpose of the footnote is to let the reader know, in as undisturbing and efficient a manner as possible, what is the source of the information in the text. Can you imagine how disruptive it would be to a reader to find footnote information thrown about randomly in each different footnote? The reader might easily lose track of the text to figure out the source. Furthermore, footnote information is really given in a sentence-like format that leaves out all the connecting words. A footnote which reads:

Lowell Thomas, *With Lawrence in Arabia,* (New York: P. F. Collier & Son, 1924), 129.

is really saying as follows:

A book by Lowell Thomas, entitled *With Lawrence in Arabia,* was published in New York by P. F. Collier & Son in 1924. The reference is to page 129.

As you can see the original footnote form simply eliminates the words which do not vary from note to note and retains only the publishing information which would vary from note to note. The result is a highly efficient form of referencing to outside sources which can be understood at a glance from the reader. In fact the history of footnoting has shown that whenever a more efficient method of footnoting surfaces, one using fewer words or text interruptions, the more efficient style is usually adopted by most academic fields. (Thus, in some publications the more efficient APA style is replacing the older humanities style.)

As a next step in your footnote study, have at hand a book which has some sample footnotes, either your outside source, any textbook or a writing handbook (such as the *Little, Brown Handbook*). Looking at a footnote that refers to an outside source, pay particular attention to the following details:

1. The ordering of all the entries; what is the guiding principle?
2. Are there any numbers in the lefthand column which precede the formal entry? What is the logic?
3. Examine the entry to answer:
   a. What is the order and type of information listed?
   b. Is the author's full name given? Is his first name given first or last?
   c. Are titles underlined or quoted? Are title of books and titles of journals handled similarly?
   d. How are volume numbers indicated?
   e. Are arabic or roman numerals or both utilized? When?
   f. What sort of publishing information is listed? Where can you find this information in the source? Is the same publishing information listed for books and journals?
   g. How are specific pages listed?
   h. Note the exact location of all periods, commas, and parentheses within the entries.
   i. What are the rules for margins?

Once you have reviewed a footnote in this detail you are ready to assemble your own footnote guide. Take some 5 x 7 note cards and make sample entries, one per card of the following items:

1. Book with one author
2. Book with two or more authors
3. Journal article with one author
4. Journal article with two authors
5. Journal article with more than two authors
6. Government publication
7. Article by an anonymous author
8. An interview
9. An encyclopedia article

Once you have an entry on each card, annotate the entry by noting the answers to the questions asked above directly on each card. The sample card below provides an example.

Example of Annotated Bibliography Card

```
last name first
   first name last        period after title
   comma between names
   period after names        title underlined
Kemler, Edgar. The Irreverent Mr. Menken.
   (Boston: Houghton Mifflin Co., 1950.
         colon after place        comma after publisher
Publishing Info.:
                                period at end
      place, publisher, year.
first line out 6 spaces, second line indented
```

Although this simple exercise should make you feel comfortable with the mechanics of footnote form, it does not answer all questions about footnotes, because the real problem of inside the text procedure still remains. Most students still have questions about when to footnote, where to put the numbers, how to handle quotations, how to refer to a source within a source, etc. Many of these questions are answered in the Appendix at the end of this text. More detailed questions may be referred to your instructor. The answers to these questions tend not to vary from field to field.

There are, however, dramatic stylistic differences of inside the text referencing which do vary from field to field or from essay to essay which you also need to master in order to have sufficient skill to document efficiently. Consider these differences among the following references:

Woolley has written a delightful book published by the Oxford University Press entitled, "Dead Towns and Living Men," in which he describes the archaeological experiences of Lawrence and himself before the World War. One story throws considerable light on . . . (a long quote follows) (Thomas, 30).

Six years ago John Ciardi inadvertently unsettled a great many poetry lovers with his analysis of Robert Frost's poem, "Stopping By Woods on a Snowy Evening" (*Saturday Review*, April 12, 1958). Mr. Ciardi's thesis was . . . (a summary follows) (Armstrong, 445).

. . . Morgan and Costil (1972) studied a group of marathon runners and found . . . (a one sentence summary follows) (Gondola & Tuckman, 1295).

Among the learning-based approaches to the treatment of anxiety which have appeared in recent years is the implosive therapy approach of Stampfl (see Levis, 1967; London 1964; Stampfl, 1967, 1968; Stampfl & Levis 1967a, 1967b). This approach is based on . . . (Smith & Sharpe, 239).

For example, quantitative solar market projections have been criticized in this journal [11, 40] and elsewhere [38]; national energy projection efforts continue to produce contradictory renewable energy projections [14, 35] . . . (Sawyer, 201).

All of these passages are making reference to outside sources while continuing the flow of the written text. Each one makes that reference, however, in a style very different from the others. First let us look at the device that you usually associate with footnotes, the footnote number. Notice that not one uses the slightly elevated number system you may be used to using. The first two models provide the reference information in a way that obviates any footnote at all. The next two use an author-date system which refers the reader to the bibliography at the end of the article, and this, too, obviates footnotes. The last does not even mention authors' names, but uses a numbering system which refers to a Works Cited list at the end of the paper. Once again, efficiency reigns in the referencing system.

The most important differences among these references, however, have nothing to do with numbers. They have to do with style. The first reference moves along in a *leisurely* fashion, taking time to include publishing information before introducing content; the fourth reference moves forward in most *efficient* manner, using a list to condense several references. The first reference makes the *personal* judgment a feature of the reference; the third is strenuously *objective;* the fifth is judgmental and critical but without any hint of personal involvement of the author. The first two references want to give the reader the *flavor of the originals* as well

7

as the content; the last three want to feature the *content of the references*. Moving from the first reference through to the last, there is a general progression from an informal, elaborated style of writing to an efficient, formal style. Each represents a choice for the writer who wants to introduce outside material.

These models represent choices and an exercise for you. With one of your outside sources in hand, 1) block off a section of that source which represents one small unit of thought, perhaps a paragraph or two in length; 2) using this passage as your target text, write up five different ways you could make reference to this passage, following the varying degrees of formality and efficiency we saw in the models we have analyzed; 3) try the same procedure again, this time referring to a passage in your second source.

Preview - Part IV
Integrating Sources into the Text

Although we have reviewed a good deal about referencing and footnoting, there remain two in-text referencing skills which need practice: writing up the outside source, and judging when to use the write up.

Once again you must remind yourself that there is always the temptation to let the outside source take over your own text. If, however, you stick to your original selection plan (Preview--Part 2), and you have control of the mechanics of footnoting (Preview--Part 3), you will remain in control. You can then move on to choose just how much of the original you want to use in your essay, and in what manner you will write it up. (For a thorough treatment of this theme see Chapter VII). At this point it will be useful for us to move along in two directions at once. We have seen that referencing can be very efficient or very elaborated (long or short); it can also be rather personal or very objective. These same two qualities may also dominate the part of the reference which describes the content of the source. For example, look at these references to the content of an article by James Armstrong who analyzed a poem by Robert Frost, "Stopping By Woods on a Snowy Evening."

In the references we shall look at, Armstrong was trying to explain the message of Frost's poem. His argument was that Frost's lines were almost identical to lines in a poem by Thomas Beddoes in which the speaker dreams of a ghostly, deathly figure. Armstrong says the comparison points to Frost's real meaning in the poem. Here are several ways to write up this reference.

Mr. Armstrong's interesting thesis was that Frost's poem did indeed contain a death wish, based on a reference to a poem by Thomas Beddoes, which has a striking and colorful resemblance to Frost's own poem. (Informal and short.)

Armstrong presents evidence of a death wish theme in Frost's poem by reference to a poem of Thomas Beddoes. (Formal and short.)

Mr. Armstrong makes a convincing case that Frost's poem might contain the hint of a death wish. After building a case for the theme by looking at other Frost poems and famous critical readings of the poems, Mr. Armstrong brings forth his finest piece of evidence, a passage from a poem by Thomas Beddoes, in which the speaker yearns for death. The resemblance to Frost's poem is dramatic. (Informal and longer.)

Armstrong analyses the death wish theme. He includes references to other Frost poems and to accepted critical interpretations. He concludes the analysis with a citation from a Thomas Beddoes poem, whose speaker yearns for death in words reminiscent of Frost's language. (Formal and longer)

. . . After Mr. Armstrong deals with Mr. Cox's responses to Frost's imagery, he turns to another convincing source. In a poem by Thomas Beddoes, "The Phantom-Wooer," Mr. Armstrong hears a striking echo of Frost's "The woods are lovely dark and deep,/But I have promises to keep/ And miles to go before I sleep." Mr. Armstrong sets the stage by saying Beddoes' speaker is the subconscious mind of a sleeping lady to a wooer:

> ....come
> With me into the quiet tomb,
>   Our bed is lovely, dark and sweet;
> The earth will swing, us as she goes,
> Beneath our coverlets of snows,
>   And the warm leaden sheet.

This is convincing evidence. (Informal and longer)

. . . Armstrong refers to Cox's treatment of Frost imagery, particularly of woods and landscapes as dark temptations. The analysis continues by reference to Beddoes' "Phantom-Wooer." The focus is on the rhythm, rhyme-scheme, and message of the lady's subconscious words to a tempter:

> ....come
> With me into the quiet tomb,
>   Our bed is lovely, dark and sweet;
> The earth will swing us, as she goes,
> Beneath our coverlet of snows,
>   And the warm leaden sheet.

According to Armstrong ". . . there is a remarkable similarity of mood and theme. . ." (Formal and longer)

There may be any number of variations along the double axes of length and formality. Notice that as the note gets longer, the part of the original source which is treated in detail gets longer, too. A brief reference can refer to a whole source on one line, while a long reference will refer to one tiny part of a source at length. Notice, also, that the same content from the source can be presented formally or informally. Finally, notice that in the long references, the author's name was referred to several times; using the name once and then using the ideas extensively is not a safe or correct way to refer to outside sources.

Now it is your turn to try your hand at referencing with varying degrees of formality and length. Choose one of your sources, read it thoroughly, and write model references according to the following scheme:

1. One sentence reference to the whole text, informal.
2. One sentence reference to the whole text, formal.
3. Short paragraph reference to an important passage, formal.
4. Short paragraph reference to an important passage, informal.
5. Detailed paragraph reference to an important passage, formal.
6. Detailed paragraph reference to an important passage, informal.

9

Once you have mastered these referencing skills with confidence, you are ready to judge when you should use them appropriately. There are two factors which help you decide: your audience and your subject. We have already discussed how the audience helps you to choose content, select language, and decide your own voice in the essay. Along with these you should decide how familiar your audience is with your source material. Notice that in the notes above, some of them assume that the audience knows the outside source and needs only a reminder, and some assume that the audience needs to be filled in about all details, and a few assume that the significance as well as the content must be explained. Knowing your audience also helps you to decide what degree of formality would be appropriate as you write these references. Would formal, brief referencing to scientific material be appropriate to your audience of sympathetic but nonexpert peers?

The second factor, your subject as you wish to present it, should help you decide further just how extensively you need to use outside sources and in what depth. In this essay try to limit your use of your two sources to three purposes: 1) adding facts or details to your general ideas; 2) adding a voice of authority to your interpretations; 3) adding a way of organizing material which you found difficult to control. Of course, in each instance, you will document the use of others' ideas in a pattern that you have practiced. Even if you are using only another author's organization of the subject, reference that kind of borrowing as well, just as we have practiced.

It is now time for you to return to your original essay, review your efforts and write the next draft. It will be helpful for you to follow these steps:

1. Reread your draft, your audience analysis, and your lists, matching content and source.
2. Thoroughly read the appropriate sections of your two outside sources; evaluate again the use of these sources for your essay; write out the content references, on cards or in your journal, as you intend to use these passages in your essay.
3. Rewrite your essay, for your audience, with a very narrowed focus, and with proper referencing.

Preview - Part V
Revision

Now that you have in hand your third draft of your essay, you are ready to write another draft!

It is usually surprising to students just how many drafts professional writers write before they are satisfied with the finished product. One art historian told a group of my students that she usually rewrites her essays at least five times before submitting them for publication. (This may be a low number for some writers.) What is she working on between drafts?

If we return to the description of the writing process, we see that it calls for rewriting and editing--as separate steps. What is the difference between these tasks? Many students know that they must check spelling, punctuation and grammar before they hand in their papers. Since anyone might do this task for them without changing (or sometimes without even understanding) the message, we might well call this activity editing. There are other changes a writer often makes to clarify, amplify or emphasize the messages of the essay; these we may label as rewriting. (In reality, the division is often not so sharp, but it will serve our purposes here.) Let us think of editing as making corrections and rewriting as making the quality of writing better. (See Chapter VIII for a more complete discussion.)

There are many, many concerns of language, sentencing and paragraphing which contribute to improving the quality of an essay, and we cannot pretend to cover them all in a brief preview chapter. We can, however, review some methods of checking your writing which will aid in its clarity and effectiveness.

A first step is to test your paper for two important qualities: *unity and coherence.* For our purposes let us agree that unity means writing so as to make one point clearly, and coherence means writing that flows smoothly from one point to the next. These two qualities should be present at every level of your paper. The whole paper should be unified if each paragraph or section is relevant to your one central idea. Test for this by writing your central idea for the whole paper in one sentence, in a few carefully chosen words. Now match this sentence against main idea sentences from each paragraph. There should be a close relationship in words and content between each pair of sentences.

You may test for whole paper coherence by listing in order each paragraph's main idea sentence (sometimes called topic sentence), and seeing if there is a flow between the sentences; does one lead to the next? Even though these sentences do not appear in sequence in the paper, they hold the paper together if they refer back to the previous topic sentence and forward to the next.

These tests for unity and coherence should also take place on the paragraph level, where each group of sentence clusters in a paragraph should be tied to a central topic sentence by language and idea, as are the spokes to the hub of a wheel; and each sentence should lead to the next, as the wheel rolls surely down a path. You will be able to test for these qualities only by careful reading of your text 1) for repeating key words (words that appear in the topic sentence), 2) for effective use of transitions (such as "first," "second," "now," "then," "although," "however," etc.), and 3) for pronouns ("their," "it" etc.) that refer back to specific nouns in the previous sentence as well as for effective use of other substitution words. You must read sentence by sentence, guessing at what the next sentence should say, and measuring it against what is really written on the page.

The next test must be for *development of ideas.* Many students feel that once an idea has been written in a sentence, the writer's job is complete. Readers, however, are not at the writer's side when the idea is written down; they cannot say "I do not understand that." As a result, the writer usually has to explain every major idea of the essay in some way. This means that each paragraph must be devoted to developing its central idea fully enough to insure no misunderstanding on the part of the reader. You can test each paragraph for development if you can recognize the difference between a generalization and specific, concrete detail. A generalization is a statement that holds together several discrete experiences or abstracts experience into an idea. Specific and concrete writing presents experience in its unique form, making us be there through the senses or understand through logic. Look at the tension between general, and specific in these two paragraphs:

> An Arabian banquet is an occasion to be remembered. After the war King Hussein entertained . . . in honor of Prince George Lotfallah of Egypt. Rows and rows of small tables were placed end to end and then piled high with food until they groaned under the weight. Eighty guests were served at one sitting and the waiters walked up and down on top of the tables, looking down at you. If your plate was not full they would slice off a slab of sheep or goat and then step over the cake and attend to your neighbor. After the first eighty had dined, the next sitting was served in a like manner (Thomas, 57).

> In every town and small city of America an upper set of families stands above the middle classes and towers over the underlying population of clerks and wage workers. The members of this set possess more than do others of whatever there is locally to possess; they hold the keys to

11

local decision; their names and faces are often printed in the local paper; in fact they own the newspaper as well as the radio station; they also own the three important local plants and most of the commercial properties along the main street; they direct the banks. Mingling closely with one another, they are quite conscious of the fact that they belong to the leading class of the leading families (Mills, 30).

In each of these paragraphs it is not difficult to locate the generalization and block off the specific details. Notice that the details occupy more than eighty percent of each paragraph, and that their wording and elaboration enliven rather ordinary generalizations. Not all paragraphs serve the purpose of developing an idea, but most of them do and, therefore, you should check each one for the tension between generalization and specific, and for the appropriate percentage of writing devoted to the generalizations and the specifics.

Another test of your writing should be with an eye toward *sentencing and word choice*. Once again, let me emphasize that one paragraph cannot even begin to cover these concerns in sufficient detail; we can merely alert you to these concerns. In every paper, no matter how scientific or academic, you have the opportunity to make your writing clear and strong by carefully choosing your words and structuring your sentences. Consider the language of the sample paragraphs. In Thomas' paragraph "groan" and "slab" do much to make the details visual and powerful. In the Mills paragraph the cluster of similar words--"own," "hold the keys," "decide"--underscore the main idea. Change those words, and the message would not be as clear or strong in either paragraph.

Consider the sentencing of the Mills example. The middle sentence holds all the details, linking them together the way the lives and status of the upper classes are linked together in the small towns Mills describes. It would have been easier for Mills to write in short sentences and with periods rather than semi colons, but the pattern in which the structure reinforces the meaning would have been lost. In many of the papers you write, you may not feel it is appropriate to reach for the most colorful language or sentencing, but do not settle for the first or easiest choice either. Clarity and strength in writing take a little work and a lot of rewriting. (For a thorough treatment of this subject see Chapter VIII.)

Once you have rewritten your paper with an eye toward unity, coherence, development, word choice and sentencing, the paper should be ready for editing and a final proofreading. Although these are usually the last steps of writing any essay, I am going to ask you to perform one last analytical task while your paper and sources are in hand. Ken Bruffee suggests that students can learn a lot about writing if they are able to describe writing in two ways: what it says and what it does. In other words, he wants students to be able to explain the content of the writing and the strategy of the writing, paragraph by paragraph. There are many ways to describe what strategies are used in the paragraphs of an essay. In a simple essay, for example, the opening might present an opinion or a statement of belief. The next paragraph might present a reason to support the opinion. The next paragraph might present another reason, and so on. This is a very simplistic level of description, and will not afford much insight into options in writing. In our Preview sections we have used other terms to discuss your essay. We said you might write the "background" of your subject, or the "significance" of your subject. These lead into another descriptive scheme for writing which also includes "explanation," "good and bad factors," "application" and other informative strategies. Still another descriptive scheme might note the source of information, such as "cite personal experience," "cite known authority," "cite first hand witness." Finally, most writing teachers prefer to describe writing by identifying rhetorical strategy, including "narration," "description," "analysis," "classification," "comparison and contrast," and "definition." There are probably other schemes which could be devised to describe how an essay says its contents. In your journal you might try to come up with another scheme.

Once you feel comfortable with two descriptive schemes, it is time to apply the scheme to your writing and to one of your sources. In the margin of your paper make two notes per paragraph; one should note the contents of the paragraph (what it says), the other should note the strategy (what it does). Move through the entire essay, but be sure to stay within the vocabulary appropriate for the descriptive scheme you selected when you started the analysis. Try the same for one part of your outside source.

The advantages of this exercise should be felt immediately and all throughout this book. Right now you should be able to begin to read your writing for its strategic pattern, and any inconsistency in the pattern should call for swift correction. More importantly, however, as you move through the readings and writing in the chapters ahead, you will have the skills with which to describe and then imitate any kind of writing you encounter.

CHAPTER 1 - CONCEPTS AND DEFINITIONS

One writing assignment every college student expects is the research paper. Most students expect to write a research paper as an important assignment in a freshman writing course, and then they expect to use research writing skills throughout their college years and perhaps throughout their professional careers. Mastering research paper techniques, therefore, seems as if it should be an important part of a college writer's experience.

Even though college students expect this assignment, they do not welcome it, looking at it as a task loaded with frustrating searches in the library, note cards checked by the teacher, pages of writing ground out late at night, and grades based upon how expert the nonexpert student can sound without plagiarizing. I remember that when I was a freshman in college I had written only one or two research papers in high school, and those experiences had been preceded by social studies papers for which I had copied all of the information out of an encyclopedia. With these two kinds of experiences it is no wonder that I had only a vague notion of what a research paper might be in college; it is no wonder that, as I stood on the threshold of College Composition I, I trembled at what lay ahead.

I do not think my experiences nor my early concepts of research writing were unique. When I ask my students what a research paper is, they usually tell me that it is a comprehensive paper on everything they can find out about a subject. It is a paper based on information dug out of the library. It might contain their opinions, but the purpose, they say, is to use the opinions of professionals to find the right answers. When the paper is done, the students say they know the truth: they know if vitamin C prevents colds; if gun control lowers the crime rate; if abortion should be legalized.

The shocking experience for many of my students who hold to this definition of the research paper is that if they write this sort of global, source laden, simplistic paper, it will not be graded very highly nor would it be labeled research in subject area courses like psychology, sociology, environmental science, or other college subjects. It might be that in beginning courses in a subject area in college, term papers are required in which students must show a familiarity with wide-ranging subject matter, and in the Preview sections to this text we have reviewed many of the characteristics of that kind of paper. Nevertheless even these papers benefit students more if they contain the analytical techniques, the methodologies, the forms and the styles of professional researchers. The term papers will receive better grades, and the students will understand more about the nature of the subject area.

If high school term paper models will not serve you well enough in college, what, then, shall you turn to in order to master the research paper? Many contemporary teachers of writing, in attempting to answer similarly troubling questions about writing, have found some answers by asking writers *how* they do their writing rather than *what* they are writing. When my colleague, Professor Robert Schwegler, and I asked researchers how they do research, most of them described activities very different from the students' activities when writing research papers. The first thing many of the researchers did was talk--to colleagues, experts, friends, even spouses--about their ideas. As they continued their research, they continued to bring in others by talking and by having them review pieces of writing. Most of these researchers spent very little time in the library. Instead they spent time in labs, or recording field observations, or analyzing primary sources or other first hand objects as their major points of focus. Throughout their projects these researchers were very concerned about their methodology, being aware that how they analyzed their subjects was as critical as the nature of the subject itself. As a result they did not write everything they knew about a subject in one paper; instead, they examined one small aspect of a large subject. (For example, one researcher whose subject is algae spends his summer counting microscopic algae in one acid pond in Alaska; another researcher who is interested in how people respond to machines spends time observing how library users respond to one computer in the reference area of one library.) In every case these researchers were aware that they had to write up their research in a form and in language that was familiar to their audience, and they felt that their success as published researchers was due in large part to their abilities to write. Finally, most of them felt that each project tended to raise more questions than any single project answered. (For example, did the presence of one kind of algae in one pond mean it would be present in other ponds? Would the student who banged the top of the computer in the library on Tuesday bang it again on Thursday?) The final truth in any one area seemed very elusive.

If these are the activities and concerns of the researcher, then we should not be surprised that the written version of this research process is not the wide-ranging, quote laden paper we used to write in high school. The written version of the research process has very narrowly focused subjects; it has explicit (or implicit) methods statements which lead to extensive analyses; it has very predictable written structures (which we will study in this text); and it has as its audience other experts in the field who are working alongside the writer in a continuing search for a better understanding of the subject.

Does this sound very puzzling or abstract to you as an inexperienced college writer and researcher? After all, how can a beginner talk to experts like an expert? How can a student in a writing class count algae in an Alaskan pond? The answers are that even though we are not based in Alaska we can come to appreciate the research process of researchers everywhere and we can study one product of that research--the paper. We can imitate in small scale some of those processes by learning to count or observe and analyze; we can talk to the researchers about what they do; we can look at how they have written up their findings, looking for conventions of form and language so that when we write up our studies in miniature they have a structure and a vocabulary familiar to the expert reader. If we study the process and product of research we will understand and be understood.

Exercises
1. Write an entry in your journal which describes the research papers you have written until now. Try to describe the papers and the steps you went through as research.
2. Interview researchers in fields you may be interested in studying. Find out what they do, how they do it, and how they write it up. Report to your class on your findings.

Your Experience as a Researcher

Another comforting aspect of our study in this text is that I believe you do have useful research and writing experience to draw upon as college freshmen. Most of you have had science courses with laboratory sections. Most of you have had to write up lab experiments, perhaps by filling in work sheets or following an outline dictated by the teacher. These lab reports may seem a far cry from a full-blown college research paper, but, in fact, they give us more insight into the process and product of academic research than those other high school models.

First, the lab report is a record of a process; it is a record of what you did to, or what you observed about, a particular thing. (Perhaps you had to add one chemical to another and record the result; perhaps you had to do as I did in botany--count the numbers of blades of grass in 1 square inch over several areas on a lawn and make a prediction about the quality of the lawn.) Everyone else in the class carried out the same procedure and filled in the same form. (We had a lot of sore knees that day!) Thus, the first quality about most lab work that we can generalize is true for most research is that it is an active process in which you will be doing something--measuring, analyzing, probing--to something under study, be it a chemical or a blade of grass, a person or a painting. Furthermore, whatever it is you are doing, we may call your methodology, and this methodology, in large part, leads to another important generalization about research: it is meant to be repeated. Anyone who follows the method you followed upon the same subject matter should come to the same conclusion you came to in your probe. Not only that, the very tight form of the lab report makes sure this is possible! Without swamping the lab instructor with questions, thirty-five students can repeat a research process, and even account for varied results, by following the methodology and filling in the lab report. Thirty-five students will work their way through an investigation finding, within a reasonable range, the same conclusion about a subject. We will study more about methodology in later chapters, but for now you should begin to think of methodology as a key step in any research process, one that insures predictability. This predictability about the things of this world is one way of knowing about a subject.

Finally, your experience with the lab report will lead us to another insight about academic research that should help you as you gain experience in reading the research of others and in designing and writing your own research. In the lab experiment you usually found yourself testing an hypothesis by following a certain method; this format for lab research is so universally true that, in a narrow sense, we might say that testing the hypothesis is the purpose of many a lab experiment or research. (We will explore the nature and definition of hypothesis in the next chapter; but for now I assume we can hold to a simple concept of a hypothesis as a statement of probability to be tested by the research process.) As your research reading and experience grows, you will see that many researchers seem to retest the same or similar hypotheses on the same or similar subjects. This is so universally true that retesting, remeasuring, or rediscovering become the purpose of another activity of researchers. In this way researchers move towards a feeling of certainty about their subject. (For example, if other researchers on the edge of Alaskan acid ponds find similar patterns of growth among algae in acid ponds, then such corroborate evidence might move them towards certainty about one result of acid water environments universally.)

Academic Research

In the world of academic research, testing and retesting of hypotheses are often such important activities that the records of these tests--the papers, reports and essays--fill volumes and volumes of journals, take up conference time, and often find their way into government reports. The results of some of these tests sometimes also find their way into newspapers, if a reporter deems them somehow newsworthy. Medical "breakthroughs," surprising technological applications and "advances" in education tend to receive this kind of coverage. Local newspapers have started to devote weekly supplements to such reports, complete with interviews and local color, such as eye witness lab visits. This is often how the public keeps track of the space program, computer technology, robots and cancer.

Academic researchers, however, look to these tests and retests for very different reasons. They want to know the refinements in methodology which will enable them to continue with their own research. They want to keep track of the unanswered questions, the gaps in the results, the developments in related areas which might help their own fields. They also depend upon these written records to keep them involved in the "social" networks of research. But volumes of results, by themselves, constitute nothing more than volume of results, waiting to be integrated into an organized system of meaning. If enough information has been generated through testing and retesting, a researcher in the area, reading about these tests, will often begin to see a pattern, a chain of related findings, that organizes the entire field. In this way researchers edge their way towards theory. (Researchers in Rhode Island, for example, after reading the concrete data generated from Alaskan pond life studies, might now be ready to abstract a full picture of acid rain biology.)

One of the ways researchers look for patterns in their fields is to conduct a review of the research, watching for a theory emerging or a new direction taking shape. At some point in the process of all specific research there seems to be this step into the abstract which moves towards the presence of theory. Theory making, then, is another purpose of research. There are several forms of research papers which serve the purpose of theory making, each having their own structure and their appropriate language. We will review one of the most obvious kinds, the review of research.

Theory making can have very powerful results. If the emerging theory seems to be right, if it helps to give meaning to every observation, it seems to take over and dominate the way we see reality. Darwin's theory of evolution, for example, so powerfully organizes so much of the evidence in the natural sciences (and the human sciences, too) that even the lay public understands that life is a struggle for existence where the strong inherit the earth. Marx's economic theories gave a structure to the chaos of events in Europe in the late nineteenth and early twentieth century, so that governments have been shaped by those doctrines. In much less dramatic ways most of the information we receive in classroom lectures are molded by theory formed on the basis of testing and retesting. Geography, now taught from the theory of tectonic plates, economics, now taught through mathematical models, and composition, now often taught from process-oriented theory, are three academic teaching areas dramatically revolutionized by theory.

Theory, however, is not the end of the research process. If the theory is accurate, it helps guide further research. The theory of evolution has suggested and guided research projects in the natural sciences; B. F. Skinner's theories of behaviorism have helped psychologists to state hypotheses, design tests and interpret results. Theory is needed to step back to the concrete; the application of theory often becomes a purpose of research. It, too, has a methodology and an appropriate paper structure which we will study in this text. When we read these papers, we see theory put to the test. And we might also see where the theory does not hold, where now--emerging results and new data will call forth new hypotheses, starting the cycle of research once again.

It is our experience that much of research seems to proceed within these parameters. Testing a hypothesis; corroborating or refuting an hypothesis; reviewing the literature; and applying a theory. Each of these goals of research seems to carry with it a particular paper structure that makes the process and the content available to us, so that we, as beginners, may read, understand and imitate in rudimentary ways these research projects, and write up the results.

These ideas about research, the emphasis I have given to methodology, and even the language I have used--testing, measuring, and similar words--may seem appropriate for scientific investigations only. However research in the social sciences often employs the same vocabulary and methodology; and research in the humanities, while not using this vocabulary, still carries out a process of probing a subject, testing insights about a poem or a painting, following a well-known or new train of thought about an historical event, until what the researcher "sees" in the subject can be "seen" again and again by others. From this perspective, all academic research shares in approach and purpose: which is nothing less than an ever-refined process of trying to understand a subject.

Exercises

1. As a class, identify the major areas of academic research. Have class members speak to professionals in each area; find out the kinds of questions they research, their methods, their writing formats.
2. Bring to class a science supplement of a local newspaper. Look at the articles which describe the research activities of professionals. Match these descriptions to the analysis presented in this chapter.
3. Write a paper or a journal entry which defines academic research using the material gathered from interviews.

Application

The second half of each chapter of this book, will be devoted to helping you to apply the concepts discussed in the first half of the chapter. The first half of this chapter, for example, discussed some of the activities of the researcher, and the connection between those activities and the written record of that process: the research paper. The second half of this chapter will guide you through perceptual activities to help you see the link between the process and product of research.

Referring, again, to lab experiments, think of the written product which follows those experiments. What are the parts that usually must be written: the hypothesis, the materials and method, the results and discussion or interpretation, the conclusion. Think about this list of parts. They are not merely parts of a paper; they are the parts of the process of research. Any researcher, such as the mathematician contemplating the spots of the leopard, spins out an hypothesis, perhaps that a predictable chemical wave makes those spots. He might, then, design a procedure for testing that hypothesis. Perhaps a chemical test is called for; perhaps a mathematical approach; perhaps a computer simulation. The results he finds from that experiment must be studied, interpreted, and finally evaluated in light of the original hypothesis to bring the experiment to a conclusion. The write up we listed above follows these very steps, doesn't it? If we can learn to read the product for these important step/parts, if we can critically and analytically review each step/part as a record or a *representation* of an investigation, then we can begin to think and write and communicate among experts.

The first step is to become a critical reader and researcher. When you read a research paper, you should identify the parts of the process we have been discussing, from hypothesis to conclusion. Perhaps, too, you will identify other parts of the research paper which we have not yet mentioned. After reading for these parts, you will begin to evaluate each of them, but the first step is recognition. Your instructor will present several samples of research from various academic fields, and perhaps you can supply some samples from journals or texts that interest you. Read through these samples, and identify the parts we have listed, deciding if the following analysis applies to your reading.

Reading Journal Research

The first element you, as a critical researcher, might look for as you read these papers is the *hypothesis*. Remember, we tentatively defined hypothesis as a statement, insight, or generalization which is to be tested by the methodology. In scientific papers, this might appear early in the paper or even in a short paragraph preceding the paper called the abstract. In other cases the hypothesis might not appear until the end of a long introduction. Sometimes the hypothesis is not even stated; it is implied. That is, the information in the opening paragraphs lets you know rather clearly what issue is being examined, but the writer, perhaps for the sake of style, does not spell out the hypothesis in one sentence. Nevertheless, critical readers should form the sentence for themselves. Only then will you be able to ascertain the purpose of the research you are reading, and only then will you be able to ascertain if the writer has done justice to the hypothesis.

As an analytical reader, you might also notice that the opening paragraphs of a research paper usually contain the *background information* about the topic that helps give meaning to the hypothesis. For example, in a botany class I performed an assigned experiment with the hypothesis that a plant would grow upwards no matter where the source of light is located. I started the experiment with the feeling that the instructor knew the outcome, and that this was an exercise for me to repeat something or to test an hypothesis that he knew already, but as I wrote up the background information I realized that there were several theories to account for the plant's behavior, and the immediate explanation of stem movement was still open to question. The purpose of the assignment was to have me enter the professional debate through my own model of the experiment and perhaps add credence to the most plausible theory. When I wrote the background for that paper I had to present *a quick review of the recent research* so as to make clear *the theoretical debate* and *the role of my experiment.* In this simple way the experiment became a real research project.

Since this background portion of the paper provides the context for the hypothesis, it is an important part for you to identify and understand. This write up may take the form of a quick review of the research done to date, or just as frequently be a short narrative of how the issue arose for questioning. In effect, the writer is justifying his research by establishing the importance of his topic, the context of his hypothesis and the openness of his questions. Within any topic, there are some issues which are open to question and some which are not; some issues which are currently debated and some which are considered out of date; some issues which cover a tiny aspect of a topic, some which cover a broad aspect. All of these things are established by the author in those opening paragraphs, and you, the critical reader, are aware of them, because it helps you to design your own research and to evaluate the worth of others' research.

Next you might turn your attention to the *list of references* found at the end of the paper. These references also cast light on these same issues; the list is an acknowledgment of the context within which the research has proceeded. As you review this list you can easily judge the material with which you must be familiar if you, too, want to participate in the current debate; once you pursue some of the reading on the list, you might judge if the writer has brought in extraneous material or if this writer has brought out different aspects of a topic by reviewing unusual references. Eventually, you will be able to judge the depth or adequacy of the background material itself. At first you may feel unqualified to ask such questions, but the process of putting together your own satisfactory research paper will make you equal to the task.

As you continue to read through a paper you might next peruse the *conclusion*. In the concluding paragraphs, the writer will often return to the issues raised in the opening paragraphs. It is in the conclusion that the author might attest to whether or not his hypothesis has been supported, acknowledging any limitations which may have arisen from the process of the study itself. It is not unusual, for example, that in beginning experimental psychology classes the student repeat the experiments in perception that experimental psychologists performed many decades ago. As they perform the research and experiments, these students find that their results are often quite different from those of the early experimenters; did those students make new discoveries?; did they disprove the founding fathers of experimental psychology? Probably not. They probably did not control the experimental environment as accurately or as carefully as did their predecessors, and arrived at different results. These procedural variations and any other qualifying information are usually acknowledged in the conclusion. It is from this information, found in the conclusion, that future research may proceed. In fact, in many science and social science papers, the conclusion contains suggestions for more research, for new beginnings, or the call for more information. This is why much of research are merely steps towards an ever elusive point of truth or finality.

In the humanities, on the other hand, a paper may have a much more final ring to its conclusion. The humanities paper often closes with a deliberate return to the opening context of the debate or the larger issues which surrounded the hypothesis, giving an emphatic tone to the concluding paragraphs. Look at the closing lines of this close-up study of one Hemingway novel:

> . . . Hemingway's first book reflects the central intellectual and esthetic concerns which dominated his life and writing from beginning to end. . . Better than any other single work, . . . the unified whole of *In Our Time* introduces Hemingway's world and the art in which he creates it (Burhans, 328).

In this passage even though only one novel is studied, the author is reaching for significance by turning to a very broad context. These sound like the final words on the subject. Often this is good concluding style in the humanities.

In spite of the fact that this passage sounds as if it is attempting to end debate on a subject, most papers in the humanities also generate more research, which either takes issue with the paper or continues in the mode begun by the original paper. Understanding and reading for these qualities in the paper are very handy, because by taking note of the specific topic and its final context as presented in the conclusion you, as critical reader, can often find a point of departure for your own research.

Overview of Critical Reader

You should take a step back at this moment to see the critical methodology being suggested in this section of the text. In order to use the insights about research we discussed in the first part of this chapter, I am suggesting that you look at the research of others to see the process in action. When you read, take note of:

1. The abstract and opening sections for hypothesis.
2. The opening section for background information, including context and areas open to debate.
3. The closing sections for a quick sense of support for the hypothesis, of the range of background materials, of the final context and of the direction you might take in your research.

21

Of course there is much more to read in a research paper but look at all we have gained by careful analysis of the introduction, conclusion and bibliography.

Reading for Purpose

Although you are probably ready to surge ahead into the "body" of the paper, there is one more bit of analysis that will help you get your foot firmly in place when walking through professional research. The reading method we have reviewed should help you ascertain the "purpose" of each research paper based on our earlier discussion of our four categories:

> testing an hypothesis: the purpose is to use a methodology to test a narrow generalization within a subject area that is open to debate.
>
> refuting or corroborating the hypothesis or test: the purpose is to repeat a method or finding to clarify previous research.
>
> review of research and/or finding theory: the purpose is to survey, organize, and clarify previous research, and establish future direction.
>
> applying theory: the purpose is to use the principles of established theory to lead to or test an hypothesis.

Identifying one of these purposes per reading should help you pull all the readings together, see the research field in action, and help you design your own project.

Final Thoughts

We have now finished one part of our journey through the process and the product of research. At this point you might feel that it is premature to worry about the process and burdensome to carry out such extensive analyses of research materials laid out in this chapter. On the other hand, I am sure you also are ready to advance beyond immature ideas and projects. I am sure you are ready to do more than just repeat the ideas of others. I am sure you are ready to find and test your own ideas. These habits of critical reading and thinking will help you do just that. They will start you on a path toward your own research projects. They will serve you well throughout this course and throughout your college career. Although now they seem a burdensome task, with a little practice they will become very handy habits.

Exercises
1. Reviewing the Application section of this chapter, make a generalized outline (or a descriptive outline) of the parts of a laboratory report. Use the chart at the end of this text.
2. Using a sample of a scientific paper distributed by your instructor, make a descriptive outline and a content outline of the paper.
3. Write a descriptive outline and a content outline of a humanities paper. Write a journal entry which compares the descriptive outlines of the scientific and the humanistic papers.
4. Drawing on the chapter, what purposes may be assigned to these sample papers? How do you know?
5. Write an essay which compares your short term paper, written for the Preview sections, with the paper samples outlined in the exercises #1-3.

CHAPTER II - HYPOTHESIS AND A REPORT
IN THE NATURAL SCIENCES

DDT is harmful to people and pets.
Acid rain from the mid-west is wiping out the forests of New England.
Type A personalities have heart attacks.
Beethoven was the greatest Romantic composer that ever lived.

Can statements such as these be hypotheses for research papers? Haven't scientists already proven the first three of these statements, and isn't the last statement merely an accepted fact?

The answer to all the questions is no; these statements would not be appropriate as research hypotheses nor are any of them proven. Academicians are interested in these issues, and they have done much research in these areas, but as statements which are to be found in academic research papers, they are inappropriate. They are inappropriate because they are written in a way which makes the research process difficult or impossible. It is our task in this chapter to explore the beginnings of the research process and writing as they are focused around the hypothesis and then discuss some practical steps for you to take as you get started on a project. As a first step you must, of course, find a topic (and there will be several steps in this chapter which will help you find topics), but you will save time and gain understanding if you first understand more about hypotheses. (Note: The concepts about hypotheses discussed here are meant to be general and cross-disciplinary, and, most of all, functional for writers. For our purposes it is not necessary to draw upon special issues of math or logic, such as null hypotheses, to introduce students to beginning academic writing.)

In the previous chapter we defined hypothesis as the central statement(s) which the researcher is testing and investigating. The hypothesis is the heart of the paper, and it is the first item we look for in the paper, because in it we may see what is the narrow subject, what is the test or analysis and what is a possible outcome. In other words we can see the whole research process in one expression. Without an hypothesis, stated or implied, a paper is usually not a research paper. We might be able to gather all sorts of interesting data and information about a topic, but the transcribing of these materials will not make a research paper.

Let's look at some concrete examples to see how a carefully worded hypothesis can transform a project, to see how a research paper takes shape only when these data and information are used to test an hypothesis. For example, if you were interested in school truancy, you might take yourself to the library and find out lots of interesting facts about the numbers of truants, and what areas suffer high rates of truancy. You might even list opinions of authorities on causes and cures. Such a list of numbers and quotes might be very informative, but at this point the only thing you are ready to do with this material is repeat it, as a school child who can list all the states' capitals; impressive, but--so what? What are we to think about these facts and opinions?

If you take a natural next step with the material, you will probably review and evaluate it and begin to decide which interpretation sounds reasonable, which opinion you might agree with and which you doubt. In terms of our example on school truancy, you might decide that the expert who said the figures mean that school truants will become criminals holds the right opinion. If you write a paper at this point, the kind of paper you might write might be labeled an argument, because you will probably want to convince the reader that your opinion is right or that he should take some action in light of your opinion.

The academicians, on the other hand, will move in a different direction. They may not be as interested in final conclusions as in the raw data; they may not be as interested in the principal's interpretation as in the numbers of truants in that principal's building. They may want to look at raw material as guided by the boundaries of a particular theory; the sociologist may look at the behavior of the truant in a group, while the medical scientist might look at body chemical reactions of age groups. Many academicians are interested in explaining, predicting, and manipulating the raw material; they, therefore, must spend much time observing, or listening or recording information, looking for discernible patterns of behaviors, looking for the sensible regularities of phenomena. At any point the academician might put his hunch, this statement of predictability or insight, this guess into the nature of things, into one sentence: the hypothesis.

Let us therefore begin to think of a hypothesis as an informed guess--about a problem or phenomenon which the researcher is now ready to test or explore or examine in a paper.

From this perspective, one source of hypotheses is the world of experience, as filtered through the eye of an academic researcher. Although we may not consider ourselves at this time expert enough to form hypotheses relevant to academic research, we can appreciate the search for hypotheses when we see it, and even begin to imitate the appropriate activities in the most rudimentary ways. For example, we might reconstruct the thought processes at work in the search for a thesis in a model paper provided by your instructor.

Exercises
1. What might have been the real world situation that prompted this research?
2. What are the hypotheses being posed in this paper? What effects do the various discussions in the paper have on these hypotheses?
3. What might be some of the follow-up hypotheses and research?
4. How might nonacademic readers view research in this area? In your journal write an entry which speculates how a newspaper might cover this report.

More About Hypotheses

If the academician proceeds about research in an exploratory, investigative manner, ready to put an idea to the test, then there emerges some natural limitations when the research takes shape. Of course, these limitations serve to shape the hypothesis.

Let us turn once again to the example of school truancy to find some of these limitations. Suppose an expert in education becomes familiar with the patterns and behaviors of school students, truants and non-truants, interviews dozens of students, their families and friends, and observes their behavior in different places; that researcher might well come to feel that when the school has a positive and extensive influence on its students, truancy decreases. This researcher might pose the following: "School truancy might be reduced by a longer school day and expanded school services." How can this researcher proceed? The statement must be put to the test.

I am sure that each of us can appreciate the difficulty here. The tasks suggested by such a wide-open statement are enormous. How much longer must the school day be? How many services? What types of services? What measures of truancy and effectiveness should be used? How long should the test continue in order to see permanent change? How many students? How many schools? Obviously, the test and its methodology will have to be carefully worked out; our concern right now is that the *hypothesis* relevant to that research project must *suggest the methodology* and be accurate for that project. In other words, in this project school truancy, only one school might be involved with a limited group of students as subjects. The hypothesis, therefore, must be unique to that project; perhaps it might read: lengthening the school day by 2 hours to include career counseling and self defense classes correlates with a reduction of school truancy in one inner city school.

Such a project could involve a long period of time, many people, and much effort; it may even represent a breakthrough in its results. Yet, by looking only at the hypothesis, the project seems very narrow in aims and significance. This is very revealing for us as writers. For our purposes we conclude that hypotheses should be tied to the particular projects which are really involved in testing of a hypothesis, predictive of its narrow aims and of its methodology. In each statement we hear not only the topic (school truancy), but also that of some sort of test or analysis will be conducted (changing school hours), and some outcome anticipated (improved attendance or new understanding). It is with these kind of statements that research begins.

Exercises

1. Think about the subject of teen-age drug abuse. In your journal list all the relevant issues you can think of and list all the parts into which this large subject can be broken.
2. Select 5 issues or parts from #1 which seem appropriate for academic research as we have discussed it in this text. For each try to write an hypothesis using language which would imply or explain the methodology which would test the hypothesis.

Another Source for Hypotheses

In this discussion we have explored how experience leads to hypothesis formation. Another source for hypothesis formation, however, is the written record of others' research found in everything from lab reports to professional journals to letters among colleagues. These written records contain the suggestions for hypotheses.

Remember that in Chapter I we said that the introductory material of a research paper establishes the openness of the question and the frame of reference. It is this introductory material that is saying, yes, those of us interested in this topic (i.e. school truancy) would like to know more about this aspect of it (i.e. its tie to school hours). We might also be hearing that this open question needs more study; it is important to know more about it for large or small reasons, and this places the question in a frame of reference or context. (i.e. School administrators would find the question important to raise morale or to be more effective; parents might find the topic important for other reasons.)

Clearly, an important source for an hypothesis derives from what is being debated among those knowledgeable in the field. So the academician is able to locate where the debate is occurring in his area of interest by looking for discrepancies, pieces that do not fit as he reviews others' research. We will review this step of starting up research when we turn to library activities. For now, however, it is essential to understand that the research begins with a perception of a problem, a piece of knowledge out of place, a nagging bit of information that calls attention to itself; when the academician turns attention to this problem, the hypothesis becomes the means by which a step is taken from the known to the unknown. The academician wants to turn his attention to the creation of new understanding.

Let's use the topic of school truancy to generate another example. Suppose a statistician, looking at the records of school truancy, notices certain trends over time. The statistician formulates the idea that truancy increases during periods of economic hardship. Our researcher might well proceed to extended studies to test the notion that there is a relationship between truancy and economic stress. Now let us suppose that according to others in the area such a relationship is well known among educators. This interaction with the knowledge of others helps lead to a reformation of the project, for the statistician is not interested in redoing the work of others unless one of two situations exist: an inconsistency in past data or a need for more data to support some tentative conclusions. If this is not the case, then our statistician wants to move into a less agreed-upon area of interest. Perhaps combining known ideas will lead to this insight: "During periods of economic stress those school districts which spent more on services showed reduced truancy data"; perhaps bringing in information from other fields opens new ideas. Whatever the direction, the sources for the hypothesis are the ideas of the research community at large; the hypothesis is derived or emerges from the works of others but it is also the statement which solves the community's questions by moving into new knowledge.

It is important to keep this function of the hypothesis in mind when formulating a project and when evaluating the research of academicians. Individually, hypotheses of sociology or microbiology or any other field may seem hopelessly minute or insignificant. They may also seem very unoriginal because often the hypotheses come from works of others or from the next step in the works of others. Much academic research may seem even unexciting, narrow and derivative, but when seen as a means of moving from the known to the unknown we can appreciate how tentative and careful such steps must be. Finally, getting used to seeing the insights, writings and works of others as a community effort to extend knowledge gets us used to the mentality of the academician.

Exercise

1. Suppose that in research about male-female differences three reports showed that males in college classes are much more verbally active and aggressive than females. These reports showed that males answer more questions interrupt more female classmates, and they confront female instructors more than male instructors. What follow-up hypotheses might you generate from these reports?

More Limitations on the Hypotheses

We have now reviewed two sources of hypotheses, experience and reading, and we know some of the conditions which serve to limit the way hypotheses are written (through methodology and past findings). Academic research is limited, however, not only by method and hemmed in by the research community, but it is also limited by academic discipline.

In most academic research the context or frame of reference is given to you by the course you are studying. Each general academic area, science, social science and humanities, as well as each particular area, psychology, art, physics, etc., has its own approaches to topics and its own ways of asking questions. In other words these areas provide contexts which can guide you to useful hypotheses, especially if you match the approach with your own area of interest. For example, many of the students in my writing classes write about the difficulty of adjusting to college life. Some of these students have gone beyond merely describing their problems and crises to doing research into the problem. They soon find themselves working within academic disciplines, asking questions and forming hypotheses appropriate to these areas. One student, a teen-ager, began his study of adolescent crises after he read a short story about a first romantic crush. He read many short stories about late adolescence, and finally wrote about three kinds of adolescent crises found in the stories of James Joyce.

Here is another example of how a student started with personal experience, and pursued a project shaped by an academic perspective. This student was surprised by his friends' difficulties in adjusting to college life. At first he labeled it an adolescent crisis, but, after much thought, decided that some of the complaints of freshmen (especially about food) and some of the anxiety of the first semester in college were really expressions of homesickness possible at any age not just adolescence. He finally designed a study about the anxieties of freshman year as a manifestation of homesickness. In his study he took a psychological perspective, using a related theory of behavior and a questionnaire. He could have chosen a literary or scientific or other perspective. Questions from these areas could well have shaped a related research project. In the end, when he reviewed his results, this student understood that academic research sheds narrow bands of light on large areas of concern.

Since each academic area gives its own peculiar perspective on issues of broad concern, some of my students who are just beginning research become slightly disillusioned. They had hoped that after a long research paper or two, they would really know the final answers to issues (such as abortion) that had puzzled or troubled them. Now we seem to be saying that few "large" issues can be fully settled. Often we must learn to accept tentative conclusions and qualified results or to spend time putting small pieces of research into a large pattern. In the mean time you should become familiar with the kinds of questions asked by each academic area, because this will allow you to choose the approach that will most satisfy your interests, while also helping you to form an hypothesis.

Exercises
1. In your journal list four academic disciplines and state how each might hypothesize about the rising college drop-out rate.
2. Using some of the information gathered from your interviews of academicians, ask other academicians in other fields if they could possibly investigate the same things and how. Summarize your findings in a journal entry.

Hypotheses and Causality

The links between events, between circumstances and outcomes, between beginning events and end results, are probably the most interesting kinds of research topics for students and for many academicians as well. (For example, does lack of gun control laws cause high crime rates?; do acid emissions from a factory in Detroit lead to a dead tree in Maine?; did unhappiness in the adolescence of Toulouse-Lautrec lead to great art?) Most of our activities in life presuppose causal links, and great breakthroughs in research have come with the establishment of causal links, yet it is exceptionally difficult to prove decisively what links one action in a causal way to another.

Many a philosopher from Hegel to Kierkegaard, have shown that what we assume to cause an action cannot ever be proven to be true. We may say, for instance, that if billiard ball A strikes billiard ball B, B will roll away. We can do this enough times so that we may finally say that it will always happen, but we can say that ball A caused the movement of ball B? No, we can only say that a succession of events occurred, then another succession of events occurred. At this point, the philosopher and the researcher agree that when the same events happen often enough, sequentially repeating themselves, contiguously in time, seemingly predictably, we are ready to take the leap of faith which assumes causality. We look for causal links because they explain what otherwise might be mysterious or absurd, but those links are really assumptions; they are a human necessity but they are not a human certainty.

Tolstoy adds a related insight to this issue of causality when he discusses the falling of a ripe apple.

> When an apple has ripened and falls--why does it fall? Is it because of the force of gravity, because it is dried by the sun, because it grows heavier, because the wind shakes it, or because the boy standing under the tree wants to eat it?

Tolstoy, in discussing the mystery of causality, brings to light the multiplicity of causality. He sees in the simple falling of an apple so many of the elements of nature that must be included in the causal chain that when the count is taken, the last mystical element, the boy's natural desire, seems no longer in error on that list. If so many things come to bear on the falling of an apple, what about the hopelessly entangled actions of people?

As abstract as this issue may seem, it does have its real effect in the practical realm of research and the testing of hypotheses. Researchers are very cautious and very tentative when proclaiming causal proof. In their work they know they may have simplified original conditions, so they must test and retest for similar outcomes under varying circumstances. They know that many a "causal" explanation may be replaced when other knowledge comes to light, so they are on the watch for the result that does not fit. For these reasons, hypotheses are often stated in the most tentative language: DDT is *implicated,* . . . our data will serve to *further strengthen* the hypothesis; the treatment worked with adults, *will it work* with children? This stylistic quality of the hypothesis, its tentative language, reveals the way this research must progress.

I doubt this is really a surprise to most of you if you recall how many times you must have heard that a cure for cancer is about to be found. In most cases, such an announcement is usually followed by the acknowledgement that much more testing must be done in order to find if a drug or treatment is really effective. In any one case, if A really leads to a cure for B, it is usually based on years of controlled testing, measuring and retesting. Similarly, many findings in academic research have started with simple guesses and tests under controlled conditions, gradually confirmed by numerous researchers, until all the pieces of research come together to establish a related body of knowledge, then giving birth to theory, principle or application. In this way, the sciences and the social sciences have triumphed over the difficulty of establishing causality; they have worked gradually to confirm the veracity and reliability of key hypotheses.

Some researchers are lucky to have their investigative conditions more under control than the researchers of many other fields. Social scientists of all fields find it necessary to deal in causal studies, yet their phenomenon to be tested might be highly abstract or unmeasurable, and their results may be very subjective or couched in a particular theory. Sociologists can often observe but often not manipulate their subjects. Historians cannot tinker with events; they can only reinterpret them. So how exact can their measures of causality be?

Professors of literature or art face even bigger problems in purely interpretive studies. How can we ever prove that a poem or a painting **means** anything or contains a certain message? Students often try to answer this by trying to find out about the author or the artist. Scholars, on the other hand, have observed that great works can be appreciated and understood without knowledge of the artist's life. They, therefore, often devote themselves to interpretive studies of the works themselves, presuming there must be causal links between the works themselves and the readers' responses. These scholars assume that works which have transcended time have had the greatest effects on their readers and the challenge to the scholar is to unearth the range of interpretive messages. The interpretive scholar is free to explore the meanings of the art, using hypotheses that are statements of the meanings found in the art. Hypotheses found in these kinds of interpretive studies have a style of their own which we will study in another chapter. For now we should understand that much literary and artistic scholarship is based on a presumption of a causal link between reader and story or between visual art and viewer, with an emphasis on the integrity of the work of art.

Given all of these considerations of causality, we can further understand why hypotheses are limited, tentative and cautious, rather than the sweeping discoveries reputed of science and other disciplines.

Hypotheses and Personal Judgments

Personal judgment is the broadest philosophical issue related to the hypotheses. Won't research tell us the truths we need to make personal judgments? Many students want research to settle such diverse issues as fluoride, abortion and greatest presidents. In reality, these students are asking for help with "moral," "philosophical," "ethical" or "religious" issues that hover about academic research. Research, as we are conceiving of it in this text, is so specific that researchers may, for example, discover laws of nature and apply them to design and to build an atomic bomb, but it cannot say if it would be better or not better to use that bomb. Scientists from the time of the Manhattan Project to today still hotly debate that issue. (Note: There are many academic forums for debating these "large" issues, but many academic "realms" are simply not training grounds for these judgments.)

Sometimes students expect research to make judgments about things that are really nothing more than statements about personal taste. Can we really prove that Rembrandt was the greatest painter ever? Can we really prove that President Eisenhower was a better president than President Wilson? Are apples better than oranges? The word "better" is without standard, and cast into the realm of personal preference; it is hopelessly ambiguous. When we read such a statement we immediately want to have the word "better" clarified. A writer could possibly show that Eisenhower was an excellent administrator or that Wilson was a shaper of public opinion. Either one of these ideas could be used to revise the hypothesis about these men as presidents, but could we then say that either one was a better president? Only if we agreed that skill at administration is better than skill at public relations when it comes to the presidency. (The same is obviously true for the statement, "*War and Peace* is a great novel." The word "great" is a matter of taste unless we get more specific; then the hypothesis is necessarily changed.) Questions of preference do not make workable hypotheses in academic research.

Final Considerations

During each part of our discussion about hypotheses we have added conditions that shape acceptable hypotheses, such as methodology and causality. In each case, there have been further restrictions due to the special requirements of various academic fields, and at the risk of being repetitive, we should note that research usually proceeds within the boundaries provided by those disciplines. (Remember the areas we established in Chapter 1).

In summary, hypotheses are statements; they are statements which, at first, help the researcher shape his research, and then they are recorded as the central message in the written version of that research. They start off as: educated guesses, as possible answers to questions posed within the limits of a discipline. When we read the written record of the research we usually read about those hypotheses which have been tested and supported by the research process as reliable and verifiable. And most of all, they tend to generate more questions, because they are always pushing into areas of new knowledge about which we often want to know much, much more.

That search for new knowledge, centered as it is around the hypothesis, is a slow, tentative, carefully controlled affair. This chapter has tried to review the reasons why this is the case, and if we can take time to apply those reasons to our own hypotheses, our own guesses into an area of interest, we can begin the first step into fruitful academic research.

Exercise
1. Review the sentences which opened this chapter and explain why they are not suitable as hypotheses for academic research and try your hand at making them appropriate. For each revision, explain what aspect of hypotheses is prompting you to make the revision.
2. Drawing on the discussion of this chapter, review the relationship between the subject, hypothesis and methodology, and fill out the chart at the end of this text entitled, "Chapter II--Subject-Hypothesis-Methodology Analysis."

Application

This section of this chapter is devoted to steps that you can take to shape workable hypotheses. We will also review one type of academic research paper, the laboratory report, particularly to show the centrality of the hypothesis in research. (Since your instructor will provide you with the information and data you will need to write a sample laboratory report, we will postpone the problem of choosing a topic in general until we discuss the library and its resources.)

To get started, remember the first source of hypotheses discussed, the world of experience. If we can limit that experience, perhaps in time, space or consequence, and then ask questions about the experience, we are taking the first steps. One zoologist explained that he became involved in years of research about geese while he was sitting with his lab partners and simply asking questions: why is the sky blue?; why does the grass grow upward?; why do geese fly in a "V" pattern? They chose to pursue the last question.

Let's be even more specific about these first steps. Ask yourself what areas of life are interesting? What areas do you want to know more about? Make a list; brainstorm. Next, try limiting these interests, perhaps by noting what events prompted your interest or what specific activities keep your interest alive; questions about divorce might be asked by those who have divorced parents; questions about jogging might be asked by those who are runners. As you think about these events and activities by picturing them, you can begin to ask very specific questions; Picture a child being told of divorce--what are the immediate responses? (Do they lead to specific long-term responses?) How about jogging? Picture joggers warming up; what motivates them for the task ahead? What gets them started on a rainy day? A snowy day?

Remember, from the way we discussed hypotheses above, we have to turn these ruminations into specially stated sentences. We want to push ourselves to asking questions about areas we know about, but focus on specific concerns or phenomena we do not know about. (The zoologist asked questions about an animal he knew, the goose, and he concentrated on an area he did not know about, flight formation.) The resulting sentences are possible answers to our questions, based on our knowledge of the field. I might know that, for example, long-distance runners often experience a "joggers high," and I might guess that this could keep some runners motivated even on dark, gloomy, wet days. The resulting sentence might be: Long-distance runners may be motivated to run because they get a "high."

I am sure that based on the earlier part of this chapter, you would find this sentence unacceptable for many reasons, but to modify it I want to suggest that you work with it by adjusting unacceptable language. For example, hypotheses should be specific; therefore, reconsider "long-distance runners." Are we speaking of all people who run long distances? Those training for all sports? Or just track? Or just marathon runners? Or did we mean to include the amateur runner? Or the non-competitive jogger? What distance constitutes a "long" distance? We should also probe the word "high." Do we know what is meant by "joggers high?" Is it the same as a high from alcohol or drugs? Is it psychological or physical? Is it distinguishable from the sense of well-being derived from a sound exercise program? Is "high" the right word?

Two other considerations will help us to reconstruct our sentence. In our earlier discussion, we said that our best guesses should be testable, that is, tied to methodology. We also said that we have to be wary about cause and effect statements. Both problems exist here. Do we have the ability to test for jogger's high? Is it a physiological test or a perception test? Can we rely on the statements of the runners as part of our test? And, of course, what will such a test really prove? It may show that a certain amount of runners experience some sort of change when they run more than a certain amount of miles, but is that tied to motivation? What about other factors, such as social or team pressures, desire to maintain health or the desire for competition? What about the runners who quit? Did not they, too, experience jogger's high? What about their motivation? The complexity of the causal factors creates a real need to modify the hypothesis.

Once again the method for adjusting the hypothesis should be to consider the individual words of the sentence, and add, delete or change, as appropriate. In the case of the sentence about jogger's high, narrowing the population and adding some qualifying words will do a lot towards making the hypothesis appropriate, tied to methodology and an acceptable test of causality. Perhaps it could read: "Runners training for marathon races may experience some physiological changes during daily training that may resemble an alcoholic 'high.' Such an experience may become part of their motivation to run." This cautious statement, now really a two-part hypothesis, is much closer to something really appropriate for study by several academic disciplines.

As a matter of fact, several students in a writing class did start a project about runners and joggers with the sentence about joggers high. They were interested in jogging but wondered what kept joggers' motivation so strong that they would run in all sorts of weather. One member of the group had seen a report on television about the supposedly addictive qualities of long-distance running and proposed that hypothesis. When the group set about planning out a project that would investigate runners' motivations, they immediately realized that they had no way to test for the high and they did not have access to the appropriate population, but that did not mean they had to abandon any related investigation. They finally did investigate the motives of amateur runners, starting with the hypothesis that the need for easy, inexpensive exercise was an important motivating factor. A nicely designed questionnaire revealed that previous membership on a sports team was at least as important as a sustaining motive as the desire for exercise. This group was able to investigate a subject they were interested in by formulating, then carefully modifying their hypothesis.

Skills Related to Hypothesis Formation

In addition to being aware of the language of the hypothesis and knowing the limitations of such a statement, there are other skills which you can practice to enhance hypothesizing. Perhaps these skills would better be called habits. The zoologist mentioned earlier is in the habit of questioning. He questions even the most obvious phenomenon. Researchers also are in the habit of generalizing and looking for patterns. We can offer some guidelines about questioning, generalizing and looking for patterns and urge you, too, to make them habits.

One structured way to question can be borrowed from the journalists, the five W's: what, where, when, why, and how. There are academic researchers across the

31

campus dealing with each of these questions in their related fields. An art historian is trying to date when a sculpture was made; she has it narrowed down to within two centuries. A botanist is trying to describe what is the life cycle of an acid pond? An archeologist is trying to determine where were the exact sites of Custer's Last Stand? Researchers around the country are trying to understand how cancer works. Finally, questions of why are probably the easiest to pose. Why do joggers run, even in the rain? Why did Napoleon lose Waterloo? Why is there life only on earth?

Beyond the fact that these researchers start with subjects in which they are interested and the fact that they are focused on what they do not know rather than what they do know, these researchers do not ask questions randomly. All of them ask questions from the perspectives of their own fields. The zoologist was attracted to find answers about the flight patterns of geese because he knew that was a fruitful question for his field. This knowledge of the field is something you as a beginning researcher lack in any depth, but you will begin to fill in as you progress through this book by becoming familiar with library materials and start some background reading. This might be helped along at this stage by picking some broad academic areas (such as psychology, computers, art history, etc.) and learning by interviewing and by perusing texts, library shelves, and popular specialized magazines (like *Psychology Today*), asking what are the questions appropriate to this field?

The second and third habits, generalizing and finding patterns, are aids to hypothesizing, because the answers to the questions posed by curious researchers presume that the solutions will be generally true for a range of phenomena. In other words, if the zoologist works with one group of geese and finds that eye position is related to flight pattern, then he assumes he can generalize to all groups of geese, maybe even to other kinds of birds. So, although questions should begin from specific instances, from noticing events in the world around us, from noticing the why, where, and how of the individual and specific things around us, answers, posed as hypotheses, can be sought in searching out what might be generally true (within limits) and what may even form recognizable patterns.

Looking for patterns can be aided by borrowing from the discipline of rhetoric (which we will review more thoroughly in the section on rewriting and only summarizing here). When rhetoricians want to understand something, they look at that item from special perspectives. They look for the parts of a whole unit, compare the units, and place units in groups. When looking for patterns we may use the same activities; we may list parts of the things we are studying and even parts of the subjects we are studying; we may compare similar subjects and things, and perhaps dissimilar subjects; and we may group subjects and things. In each case we should notice repeating phenomena, and striking differences; trends and directions; likeness and separateness. We are out to find the rule and make exceptions. Then we can pose hypotheses.

Exercise

1. Fill out the chart at the end of this text entitled, "Chapter II: From Personal Interest to Hypothesis."

A Writing Project

We have already investigated a format of writing which is designed specifically to test a hypothesis, the lab report. We have reviewed the parts of a lab report, and evaluated three of those parts, the introduction, hypothesis and conclusion, from the perspective of readers. Now we will shift perspectives to that of writer, and give you the material from a science project with which you might write up such a report.

Part I

When most professional writers start writing they are usually concerned with three elements, their subject, their audience and the format of their writing. Published writers of lab reports are no different; we now see how immersed in the subject a researcher must be to carry out a project; we also see that fellow professionals will be the readers of these reports, for they form the community that is doing companion research; since the researcher wants to communicate with this group as quickly and accurately as possible, the lab report format is as precise, exact and terse as possible. This model controls the writing process.

Let us review the parts of this model: introduction, hypothesis, methods (and materials), results, discussion and conclusion. (Various fields adjust the models to their own needs, perhaps eliminating methodology, perhaps combining discussion and conclusion, but we will practice all parts of the model as separate units.) For our part we might conceptualize this model as having two phases, with phase one occurring before the lab procedure, and phase two as a presentation of the results of the procedure. In this way the model may take shape in two steps: step one, project background, hypothesis and design; step two, project test, results, analysis, write-up.

During phase one concise writing is at a premium. Remember we said the opening indicates 1) the general area of interest, 2) the area where debate or a problem exists, 3) the narrowing of this area to one testable set of circumstances or phenomenon, and finally 4) the best guess at the solution, the hypothesis. Often all of this information is presented through a terse style of reference to the works of others. Amazingly, all of this information might be presented in as little as two paragraphs; the writing must be controlled, tight, and limited only to those issues listed.

For those of you who are trying this sort of writing for the first time, remember there is no leisurely, descriptive opening, no preview of the information in the results or discussion sections, and there is no description of how you, as an individual, became personally involved in the project. Think of the opening to this type of writing as serving only one purpose: to remind the reader of a shared body of information from which you can both explore new information. It is as if you are saying, "Fellow researcher, remember study x, study y? Well, problem z still exists and this is my hypothesis about it."

Before writing read the information distributed by your instructor and apply the steps we have practiced in this text:

1. Identify the academic field, the area of interest, the area of debate and the hypothesis.
2. Identify the next possible hypothesis.
3. Identify the documentation style.
4. Read the Methods section for style and content. (The methods and materials sections, at this point, need concern us only stylistically. Since we will not be doing a project at this time, we are concerned here more with the ways these sections are written and their connection to the hypothesis than with creating genuine methodology. Notice the same formal and terse style continues.)

Exercise

1. Using the materials just analyzed, write up the Introduction, Hypothesis and Methods sections of a science report for the purpose of testing an hypothesis.

Part II

The remaining part of the materials under review--the Results, Discussion, and Conclusion--constitute our second phase, calling upon the skills of analysis and writing. (Here, again, we encounter academic area variations, but we will practice basic skills involved in each section.) Your instructor has distributed the results of the test of an hypothesis. We will now review the steps towards writing up the second phase.

In the sciences and social sciences, where observation and measurement are so crucial, the test of a hypothesis tends towards that which can be measured, listed, numbered or statistically analyzed. Since the test often yields data, the researcher has two communication tasks: first, to report the data; second, to explain them. In the Results section the data are presented, and in the Discussion section they are explained. Even though these sections are stylized, there is important creative thinking behind the text. Don't let the task of writing these sections obscure that fact.

The Results section presents the data yielded by the test of the hypothesis. It must present as much of the data as possible and also tell how to read the data. Accordingly, all the data are presented in tables and graphs along with a written text that points out major features of the graphs and tables. The written text explains how the reader should read the numeric or graphic information by pointing out trends, highs, lows, significant figures, and columns which should be read together. By using this two-prong approach to reporting data, graphic and verbal, the researcher is making every effort to avoid being misunderstood. If you want to write an effective results section, you must first think and then write: think about the data, understand them, plan their presentation, and then write.

Even though the researcher now has tested the hypothesis and has some results, the report is still largely without meaning. Remember that data and numbers are neutral until we assign meaning to them. In the Discussion section, the researcher assigns meaning by bringing several perspectives to bear upon the data. One perspective is to explain how the data from this test compare and contrast with those from tests by others in the field. This perspective is sometimes so important that it can dominate the discussion, because each effective research project should be an important part of an overall search for knowledge in any area of interest. Each researcher, then, wants to know where new results fit into the overall pattern, both as a test fitting in with other tests and as a part of a large puzzle. This effects the writing style of the discussion. In this case, the reference to others' work may be more extensive, more analytical and certainly less abbreviated than those references found in the introductory section. Once again, it might be useful to compare writing styles of available models and discuss them before writing.

Another perspective that gives meaning to data is to review the findings (highs, lows, trends, etc.) with an effort to explain why the results occurred. This explanation may be based on generally accepted theory, on a careful laying out of possible causal sequences, or on explanatory insights that occurred during the data-gathering phase of the project. Clearly, this perspective allows the researcher to be insightful, creative and even speculative, and the writing style should reflect this effort. The discussion often contains the most elaborated writing of the report. The researcher takes a stand, argues for an interpretive position, and yet will not abandon the generally concise style that dominates the whole report.

Another important perspective that is brought to the data is to acknowledge the limitations of the project. Researchers are very aware that time, population sizes, measurement and observer inaccuracies, and many other factors can serve to inhibit the reliability or veracity of a project. In some fields project conditions can be tightly controlled, but in others, controls are difficult and the resulting distortions in data can effect the value of the results. These distortions or limitations are always acknowledged, not to discredit the project but to increase

34

the value of the accurate findings and to add credibility to the remaining discussion.

Once again, before you write the Discussion, think then write. Decide where your results fit and do not fit with the material provided by your instructor. Decide why the results come out the way they did and what limitations are found in the study. Plan your format and then write.

Exercise

1. Following the steps above, write the Results and Discussion sections of your paper.

Part III

Once the data have been presented and explained, the researcher is ready to judge whether or not the hypothesis has been supported. Often such a judgment signals the Conclusion section of the report (or the section may be marked with a sub-heading). Since the entire project has been designed to test a hypothesis, such a judgment is singularly important as a part of the conclusion. But we have already noted that one research project does not end the need for investigations; indeed some projects spur more questions than answers. As a result the conclusion will also point out those unanswered questions and suggest paths for future investigators. Some student writers are surprised that report conclusions do not explain how significant are the findings, perhaps labeling new discoveries that will effect large numbers of people. These writers should remember, however, that the audience of a report is a very expert, knowledgeable audience who are very aware of the significance of the project. Their interest is in the on-going search for new knowledge and directions for future research.

Exercise

1. Write the Conclusion section of your paper.

Final Thoughts

In this overview of the parts of a lab report, I have stressed the tightness of the form and style. Yet I also hope you have been able to see how this format creates moments of genuine insight for the researcher and is a format genuinely suited to its purpose: testing a hypothesis.

Section	Purpose
Introduction: area of interest, prior research, area of debate, narrowed subject.	Establish context for hypothesis.
Hypothesis, stated or implied	Present hypothesis.
Method and materials.	Explain procedure to test hypothesis.
Discussion: Compare and contrast with prior research, interpret findings, explain limitations.	Give meaning to results to help judge the test of the hypothesis.
Conclusion: Evaluate hypothesis in light of discussion; point to future research.	Evaluate hypothesis-test outcome.

Exercise

1. Revise and proofread your draft of the paper which is based on the material distributed by your instructor and upon our text.

CHAPTER III - BIBLIOGRAPHY AND A RESEARCH
PROPOSAL IN THE SOCIAL SCIENCES

One day, a student informed our class that once an hypothesis was tested and the results published, the project was over. Other researchers would have to look for other projects in other areas.

Based on the discussion of the last two chapters, I am sure you would find this kind of statement inaccurate for many reasons. We know that academic research proceeds in small segments through a large area of concern, that establishing sequence or cause is a difficult task, and that researchers work as a community, carrying on the same or similar studies. From this perspective there is bound to be, there must be, repetition. The same hypotheses are retested; the same projects are repeated; the same findings sought.

We have already discussed that testing a hypothesis is only one purpose of academic research. Much of the time a hypothesis and the test are repeated and, perhaps, refined, formulated again or readjusted. This activity, we have pointed out, is so characteristic of academic research that corroboration or refutation of a hypothesis or of methodology is a second purpose of academic research. By testing the same hypotheses and refining and improving methodology, researchers slowly inch their way toward certainty.

You can become familiar with this type of research by reading appropriate samples and by designing a rudimentary project which is derived from your reading. Your purpose will be to corroborate or add to the findings of professionals in some area of *the social sciences*. After you have read through the first half of this chapter, I suggest that you use every skill of finding a subject and an hypothesis that we have reviewed in Chapter II as related to a social science subject, and continue on to build your background and bibliography skills in an appropriate social science area. The content of this and the next chapter (Bibliography and Methodology) should guide you through this project. By the end of this chapter you will have developed a research proposal; by the end of Chapter IV you will have written an entire project in the social sciences.

Background Concepts for Bibliography

We can start by reminding ourselves that, since much of research is imitative or derivative, efficient communication among professionals is of paramount importance. In fact, research professionals operate by keeping track of each other's work. We are well aware that this exchange of information among professionals takes place through many channels, from personal conversations to letters, computer networks, papers at conferences, journal publications, and books. If we are to appreciate this aspect of research, then we must tap into the flow of information and become aware of the cues for deriving projects and planning methodology.

(Note: The discussion which follows lays out the steps you should follow to become familiar and gain access to journals for all academic areas. At the same time, however, you should also be laying out the steps for your project in the social sciences; as your bibliography practice grows your instructor will guide you towards reference area tools in the social sciences. When appropriate, use all of the skills we have discussed so far to have this and the following chapters guide you through a project in the social sciences.)

We can tap into the flow of information most easily by becoming familiar with the journals of academic fields; by journals I mean those publications which academicians turn to as the first place to publish the results of their studies. Journals are the kinds of publications appearing regularly throughout a year in which the writer is fairly certain that most of the audience are other professionals doing related projects. In some fields, particularly the hard sciences, the difference between popular periodicals and professional journals is easily determined by the type of writing and by the technical detail; in other fields, particularly the arts and humanities, the differences are not as easily noted, for academicians may also publish studies in magazines whose audience might also be knowledgeable nonprofessionals.

Tapping into this range of specialized material will call for you to have command of the following: special library skills; subject area background; a system of saving and using new information.

Special Library Skills

Since we want to gain access to the materials that will most aid our projects we must gain access to the most helpful journals by doing several things. First we must start at the right location in the library by becoming thoroughly familiar with the reference section of the library. Many of you who have written research papers in the past may have started those papers by using the card catalogue or perhaps by extensive use of popular magazines via *Readers Guide,* but these sources will not do for our purposes. We want access to the concerns of experts in the field, we want to know their research activities, and we want models of the way they write to each other, in their own language. For this we must turn to the journals by starting at the reference section. The reference section of the library contains material that, among other things, offers generalized background information (such as encyclopedias) and source access information (such as the indexes, abstracts, guides and bibliographies which list authors, articles, journals and books about your subject). It is the reference area's source access information which you must learn to use with ease and speed. The Application section of this chapter will help you take this step. (Please remember that these suggestions are made to those who have a general knowledge of the library, and who already know how to use the card catalogue and the Library of Congress and/or Dewey Decimal system. If these are not familiar, you should arrange for a library tour and orientation.)

Subject Background

Second, you gain access to those journals by being intellectually ready to use the information offered in the reference section and in the journals. Before becoming involved in a project within any academic field at the intense level we are suggesting in this text, you may feel the need to fill in background information and to gain a sense of how a field addresses itself to an issue. Carefully chosen books, introductory surveys, magazines, and encyclopedias can be helpful for this purpose, but only as an introductory step, and only as they help you save time in getting started. Accordingly, you will probably find it more helpful to start as the experts do, by talking rather than reading. Whatever the area, ask a knowledgeable person, a professor, librarian, or professional, to advise you on the best, most concise reading materials to fill in the background knowledge, the base, so that you may explore an issue within the field in more depth. Work as efficiently as possible with the materials they suggest by noting 1) the names of important experts in the area, 2) the specific areas of interest (both accepted and open to argument), 3) the key phrases and words, and 4) the titles of other books and articles. This information will guide you as you move on to in depth reading in the journals. Often you do not need to read entire books to gather this information; rather focus on the introductions, conclusions and bibliographies to books and long works, and carefully scan other sections.

Another step to be taken in order to be ready to make best use of the reference section of the library and the journals is to articulate for yourself your knowledge and your position before you start your search of others' writings. Almost everyone is influenced by information gained through reading. In most situations it is useful to blend what we read with our own knowledge, and in conversation we rarely have to articulate the sources of our ideas. In research, however, we are all aware that when we use the ideas of others, we must acknowledge the source. Many of us have been trained to use footnotes for this purpose. This task is made easier and more accurate if we keep track, from the beginning, of what we learn from our library research and what we know when we start; then we are ready to supply the documentation. We have practiced much of this in the Preview sections, and you should recall those experiences now.

Attributing sources and documentation really obscures another reason why it is important for us to keep track of the origin of our information, especially as we begin to shape our own projects. We have already said we want to address our efforts to areas under debate, and to those areas that need retesting, reexamination. In order to do that we must get a sense of where the controversy lies, where the uncertain is located. If, in a private inner ear, we can almost hear each researcher stating a position, explaining an interpretation, reviewing the hypothesis, then we have a sense of the current debate. If we can keep hold of our own ideas among the cacophony of expert voices, then at some point we, too, will be ready to add our own voice to the debate and even side with those who most closely express our interpretation.

It is important to note here that there is a subtle difference between using outside sources to repeat the ideas of others, in a term paper-like fashion, and to look at those ideas in order to shape our own projects and our own interpretations. In the first approach we are always in danger of copying; in the second approach we always have the option of verifying, reinterpreting and redesigning. Nevertheless, this can only be done if, from the moment we start our review of others' materials, even in the reference area, we always articulate where we stand, based on what and whose information.

Storing and Using the Bibliographic Information

It might be useful, therefore, to keep a running record of information sources in three ways, two of which you may already know. Note cards, which you may have already used in term papers, will provide specific information from readings. (We will review note taking and note cards in another chapter.) Bibliography cards, perhaps also not new to you, will provide source names, places, dates, etc. and summary information, and we will discuss this in the second half of this chapter. The third type of record should be "signposts" or "weather vanes"; thumbnail sketches of your knowledge in the area, other important information, ideas linked to the named source, and, specifically, what is being debated. This record might be kept in your journal. Although we have started a journal during the Preview sections of this text, your journal should now become a research diary, a place to note down insights and problems and hunches as you go through the more routine steps of research. If this record is kept, it will serve as a creative source of ideas and as a draft of your writing as well.

A final step to being ready to use the reference area productively is by being sensitive to the potential of the language of reference entries to shape your research. When you look at an entry in an index (which tends to be a list of articles in specialized fields), you are looking at what others have narrowed their efforts to studying.

The language itself can help you see where some experts are working, where questions are being asked and where you might begin to modify your own efforts. One student's beginnings might be helpful here. Joe was interested in alternate energy sources, particularly solar power. He had a brother who was installing a solar hot water heater and it seemed to Joe that those people who were installing solar energy sources in his area were similar to his brother in life style and background. He decided to see if his insight was true by moving in two directions at once: he started planning to interview dealers and consumers of solar energy, probing the personalities of solar energy users, and he started to seek out information from the library. Since this area of interest was just entering books, Joe turned immediately to indexes of social science journals. At first Joe found no entries related to his insight, and he began to suspect he would be testing a hypothesis of little relation to others' research and possibly of no validity. Finally, after much searching, he found entries entitled, "Solar Home Owners Survey," in *Solar Age* and "Solar Energy Owners and the Implications for Future Adoption Rates," in *Technological Forecasting and Social Change*. He surmised simply from the titles that questionnaires were probably used in those studies, that writers in two publications were concerned with the people who use solar energy, and that one of those journals seemed to be studying the relation between people and technology. Joe had found his direction.

From the entries in the index, Joe had gained, specifically, the name of an important journal, the names of authors to trace through other indexes and journals, and some language to play with in looking for other entries. More importantly, at his level of beginning research, Joe felt much more confident doing research with the purpose of corroborating the findings of others rather than testing an hypothesis that no other professional was testing.

As a matter of fact, Joe went on to do a very satisfying project about energy users, following the lines of thought developed during the library search. Although he was very satisfied with the outcome, the written version does not reveal the difficult time Joe had in the reference area phase of his library search. Joe had to learn to use this area; he had to find out what bibliographies, indexes and journals had to offer, where these were located, how to use them, and how to tinker with entry words and phrases until he found these two entries that opened up his study. There was creative, flexible thinking every step along the way. These are the tasks you, too, should master as you set about assembling a bibliography; these are the tasks that transform your research exercises from an assignment handed to you by your teacher to one that lets you participate in academic research.

Application

In order to listen in on the conversation of researchers we want to get at their first line of publications, the articles in journals. We usually find these by assembling a list of relevant articles (and other readings), called a bibliography, which eventually will appear at the end of your paper. If we try to find the articles by browsing through library shelves we face an impossible task, for the library will then seem a building for hiding books and journals. In fact, most libraries try to make all their materials easily available and will even aid you in finding what you need. You will cut down your searching time for our projects, however, if you think of moving through the library as you would following a map: You follow road and street signs until you find the destination. Eventually you internalize some of those signs and move through neighborhoods and areas automatically. This is exactly what can happen in library research.

In order to be efficient and thorough in your search you should take time to create these library "maps." I am, of course, using the term "maps" metaphorically, because it implies paths for you to follow through unfamiliar territory. It will be very helpful in learning bibliography skills for you to create three maps of the reference area so that you may proceed with confidence from your subject matter (your starting point) through references (the unknown area) to a journal article (your destination).

Map #1

The first map should be of the reference area in general, noting the physical location of general groups of reference works, and browsing enough in each area to know what these works can do for you. Note particularly where the following are located: 1) bibliographies, 2) indexes, 3) abstracts, 4) encyclopedias, 5) guides, and 6) handbooks. Note too, what type of information each of these references offers. You should also take time to find out about special services and techniques: 7) inter-library loan, 8) computer data bases, and 9) microforms. For each of these learn what information they provide, how they work, and if you have access to these services.

Exercises
1. Draw your first map indicating locations of the 9 listed items.
2. Make a list defining and describing the 9 listed items.

Map #2

Your second map should be a much closer view of the landmarks in the reference area. These landmarks are the specific bibliographies, indexes, and abstracts which most students across-the-curriculum find necessary to know when they do papers or projects. In this case, it is necessary to know more than location and general purpose. You should know them as you would know a busy intersection: how to get through the traffic--what are the boundaries, the population, the road bed, the traffic controls etc.--the contents, how the information is arranged, and how to read a sample citation. Your instructor will distribute a chart for gathering and storing this information for reference tools in the humanities, social sciences and sciences, which you can then have available for this and any other course. Some of the references listed are the *Essay and General Literature Index, PMLA Index, Art Bibliographies Modern*, and *Book Review Digest*. You should know your location, what information they provide, their pattern of organization, and how to read a sample entry.

Exercises
1. Create a sample list of indexes, abstracts and guides to journals in the three major academic areas. For each item list its a) call number, b) the kind of information found in it, c) how it is organized and d) one annotated citation.
2. Draw a map showing the locations of items on the list.

Map #3

As soon as you are comfortable with Maps #1 & 2 of the reference area you will be ready to use its sources to your purposes. This is the time to create your third map, routing you from your area of interest to the individual articles. When you have completed this map you will have the systematic list of journal articles, books, reports, etc. which form your outside sources for your paper: the bibliography.

This map begins with a collection of entry words which describes your area of interest so that you may get into the reference tool of your choice, such as the abstracts or indexes. For example, if you are interested in those people who use solar energy, you will naturally use "solar" as a way of getting into subject matter listings, but as Joe found, this did not always yield results. Before he even entered the library he was ready with some other entry words, such as "alternate energy sources," "energy conservation," and even "pollution." To get at the people-end of his project, he was ready with "solar users," "conservationists," and "consumers."

If you cannot come up with enough entry words or if you need some suggestions, your first stop should be *The Library of Congress Subject Headings,* a reference book that cross lists thousands of subject headings. If you look up "solar" in this book, you would find many, many other possible subject headings which you could use as entry words when you turn to the other reference tools.

Armed with your chosen area of interest, your discussion with a knowledgeable professional, some background knowledge, your familiarity with the reference area, and your narrowed subject and tentative hypothesis, and entry words, you are ready to take the next step on your map, to the indexes or abstracts in the reference area. Once again, flexibility is the key. Choose the reference tools that seem most appropriate, but be ready to make changes. Joe's project will serve as an example. Because Joe was interested in personalities of people, he thought *Psychology Abstracts* would furnish the information he needed. When he used his entry words in this book, he came up either with nothing or unrelated titles. Instead of giving up he changed reference tools, turning to *Sociology Abstracts.* It was here that he found the articles that were most fruitful for his project. You, too, should be ready to move through the reference area materials with flexibility and patience.

Once you have found relevant material in the reference tool, you must be ready to move forward and back from this point many times. If you have found sufficient references, you should proceed to locating the journals named in the entries you have listed. Locating those journals is sometimes a challenge all its own, and you should become familiar with your library's way of handling journals. At my college, for example, I would follow this procedure: First, I would take the title of the journal to a computer print-out located near the indexes and abstracts. This print-out, called the Serials List, would tell me if the library has the journal, which volumes, and where it is located. Then I would move on to the journal, using a call number, to the appropriate shelf, microfilm or reserve librarian. I keep in mind that recently dated issues might still be on the unbound volume shelves, and that some issues might be at the bindary. I also keep in mind that the library will do an internal search for materials not on the shelf and will recall overdue materials. Hopefully, I will find the journals.

If I have found only a few listings in the abstract or index, I will follow another route. First I will use the author's name to check for more articles by this same author and associated authors; second I will use the entry words generated by the one or two titles I may have in order to try searching through the index again. My third step, however, usually yields the most results. I will search out my one article and look immediately at the bibliography offered at the end of that article. Armed with these authors and titles, I will return either to the index or to the computer print-out to find more articles and journals. Occasionally, in less scholarly works, there will be no bibliography at the end of the article. In this case I scan the article, looking for names and titles that I may use as entry words to the indexes. If this, too, fails, then I must begin to suspect that for some reason I am on the wrong track with this project, and the most likely reason is that the focus of my interest is already well known. The information I seek is probably in popular magazines, books and textbooks. This does not necessarily put an end to the project, but it does mean that I must relocate my search to the card catalogue, *Reader's Guide,* and other sources of established information.

You can see that there is a general pattern of movement here, back and forth from the reference tools, in order to assemble a relevant list of readings. Such a journey takes time and patience, and will usually yield very satisfying results if you remain flexible, open minded, and creative. At any point along the way, of course, you may turn to the reference librarians for help, tapping into their existence knowledge of reference tools, journals and specialty materials. With all the resource available, if you would allot a few unhurried hours in the library, you will usually emerge with a bibliography.

Exercises

1. Review your area of interest, narrow subject and possible hypothesis, as stated on the first and second pages of this chapter. Write an entry in your journal which summarizes a) your area of interest, b) your questions, c) your narrow focus, d) your tentative hypothesis e) your specialized knowledge and access to methods.
2. Derive a list of entry words, following the suggestions in the discussion above. Select two target reference tools, and follow the entries to locate at least four promising articles.

Storing the Information

Since the information you are gathering now will be referred to many times as you continue with your project, it makes some sense to develop an organized system of storing these names and titles. Before you march off to the library with a pencil and a scrap of paper, give some thought to how you will use this information and, therefore, how to store it.

The first use is the one we have been discussing: location. Each entry that you copy from an index or other source should lead to an article or book found somewhere in the library. With this in mind you will need to store all the information which will enable you to locate the article at any time, such as call number, journal name and volume number, author and title, and page.

The second use for this information will be as the raw material for documentation in the paper, either within the text (particularly in the introduction) or at the very end as a formal bibliography. Documentation, in this case, means supplying the information that would allow readers of your paper enough detail so they, too, might find and read what you have read. Accordingly, we usually have to list author, title, journals, pages and any other publication details that will help all readers identify the same readings. Fortunately, each academic area has its own formula for documentation, a sort of code, which anyone may imitate to help this kind of communication to be accurate and efficient. It would probably be helpful, therefore, to dig up immediately a sample bibliography for your field of study and establish what sort of information is called for and in what order, following the same procedure we used for learning about footnotes in the Preview sections.

A third use of this information is annotative. As you begin to read the articles in your bibliography you will begin to make judgments about them, especially in terms of your own project. Some articles will supply very helpful information, some will be only partly relevant and some will be useless. It would probably be efficient and helpful for you to note these insights in some way, especially if you have many articles to read or if one author or journal supplies many articles. As you get on with your project it is very helpful to be able to get a quick reminder of those authors or sources which touch upon your study.

With these three uses in mind we can appreciate a system of storage that allows easy access to bibliographic information. Most professionals recommend small note cards (3x5), one per entry, on which all of the information can be stored. Many of you might have been required to use bibliography cards for term papers, and considered this the teachers' quirk, but if we remember that these cards must be used in at least three different ways, should not be lost amongst the shuffle of other papers, and can be arranged at whim (by author, or subject, or alphabet) then we can see why cards have a distinct advantage.

Arranging the material over the face of the card should also be a matter of efficiency. I suggest that each entry on the card should mirror the way the information will appear in the final bibliography. If the academic field calls for author (last name first), then title, etc., then this should be the format on the card, accompanied by all the correct punctuation (commas, periods, capitalization, etc.). Just think: if this format is laid out so early in the research project, then late that night, when the bibliography is typed, everything is in order, ready to be copied. The other information on the card, such as call number or annotations, should have a standard place, too, simply for ease of use.

Exercise
1. Design a collection of sample bibliography cards (which parallels the sample footnote cards from the Preview section), based upon a documentation system found at the end of one of your sample articles, and representative of the entries listed in Preview section 3.
2. Write four bibliography cards to match the four sample articles you have located.
3. Write a journal entry which reviews your knowledge of your subject. Follow this with an entry which describes information which you feel you still need to know. Be sure to cover: the context in which your subject gains importance; the areas of debate; an hypothesis which implies narrow focus and possible method; important experts in the area; names of key journals; materials or methods available.

Using Bibliographic Information to Start Your Project

As soon as you start assembling and storing the information that forms a bibliography, you are touching base with others who are working in the field, seeing the subject through their eyes. This offers great benefits and liabilities. One of the benefits, as we have already seen, is that you may shape your study guided by the experience of others. In terms of practical advice, as you assemble your bibliography, you should be asking yourself the following questions and more: Is my topic broader or narrower than other papers on the topic? Is my narrow subject still a point of contention in current research? Is my hypothesis still a reasonable guess? How much more specific and narrow can I make my subject and my hypothesis and still retain a viable paper? Each of these questions will start to have answers as you search through the references, with the question-answer-refinement process continuing throughout the project.

Early on in your bibliographic search you might be tempted to cut off the process and read some of the articles found in the indexes. Indulge--for a few of the most promising titles. This "preliminary reading" can be very helpful for it can confirm the direction of your bibliographic search and lead to some necessary and fruitful thinking time about your project. But do not let this reading drag on too long, nor let it lead to one of the liabilities mentioned next. Reading three to four of the most promising entries on your bibliography cards will help you clarify your own direction, confirm the sufficiency of your background in the subject area, and suggest accessible methodology.

The primary liability of finding out about others' ideas and methods is that we lose our own vision. This is especially true if we are beginners in the area and must spend much time filling in what is generally known about the area. Nevertheless, it is far better to sort out the information gathered in the reference area and in the preliminary reading by constantly asking another set of questions: what do I know? what am I learning? what or who is the source of this knowledge? what among this new information is being documented? what am I now speculating about? As suggested earlier, much of this sort of thinking can be informal, and might even be recorded in your journal. If we fail to keep and develop such a line of thought, we risk using the ideas of others as if they were our own, and we might even fall into plagiarism. To plagiarize has severe penalties in the academic world, but is a silly direction to follow when it can be so easily avoided.

Exercises

1. Reread your journal entry of the previous exercise. Next, thoroughly and carefully read the four articles related to your subject area. Now write an entry in your journal for each article which notes only that information provided by the article which fills in the gaps or answers the questions you listed in the original journal entry.

2. In your journal make an outline of Introduction and Methodology sections of a paper based upon the information gathered so far. In the margin note which outside source provides the material with which to write the full paragraphs.

Getting Ready for a Project

At this point in your studies you should be juggling many difficult issues, such as how to keep your own ideas from being swamped by others', how to keep the narrow focus of research in line with your broad interests, and how to use the ideas of others without merely copying.

The context in which these tasks assume priority is in that research in which the purpose is to corroborate or take issue with earlier research. This kind of highly derivative project, which we have evolved throughout this chapter, allows us to imitate or even simply redo the steps of others while not merely copying, if we use the Introduction, Hypothesis and Methods sections of the paper to prove the need for repetition.

Clearly the challenge in this project is to establish the need for repetition. We can begin by looking for this need when we are searching the reference tools and, especially, when we are doing our preliminary reading. If we feel a case can be made, we must use the Introduction, Hypothesis and Method sections to explain this need and plan out the project. In this way we can work with the works of others rather than merely copy them, and we can explain our insights by blending them with the practice in referencing that we gained in the early chapters of this text.

Your Introduction section, in particular, should now be adjusted to explain the need for repetition. You can explain the need for repetition by deciding if the reading suggests any of the following circumstances: 1. More data is needed; 2. Methodology needs redoing or redesigning, perhaps on a new subject; 3. The hypothesis should be tested on a new population; 4. A new background perspective leads to a retest.

We have said in the previous chapters that the introduction establishes many points: the broad area of interest, the area of debate, the narrower focus and question, and your best guess as to a solution. In the corroborative project we are now pursuing, the area of debate is sharply outlined for us: is there a need to redo the same or similar study? Using this one question as an analytical focus we can use the works of others without copying.

Exercises

1. In the material provided by your instructor, note the difference between the introductions. Which one merely repeats the findings of other researchers and which one actually uses these findings to explain the need to re-apply the method?

2. Write a journal entry which describes what need there is to corroborate previous research in your subject area.

3. Using the entry from #2 and from the previous exercise, write a draft of an Introduction for your project.

A Research Proposal

The final area of analysis at this point in your project is to note the relation between the methodology and the hypothesis in the selections you peruse during preliminary reading. Professional researchers frequently find that they have many options in methodology, choosing among questionnaires, interviews, inventories or tests, for example, in some of the social sciences. The challenge often is not designing the method but choosing the appropriate one that will truly test a hypothesis. Even though we probably will not have access to the actual methods of researchers we are reading, and even though we may not understand the technical aspects of those methods, we can usually appreciate why the method was chosen, based on careful reading of the introduction and hypothesis. If we can develop an eye for this aspect of our analysis we can proceed to the writing of our own tentative research plan.

One way to get a feeling for the choices of methods in the social sciences is to inventory the methods in the articles you are reading, and explain why those particular methods might have been chosen. When surmising the links between hypothesis and method, remember that many environmental, time and monetary factors help in the choice of method (such as the location of the researcher, the cost of the procedure, etc.), as well as the appropriate design of the method itself. (Much more is said about this in Chapter IV.)

Once we are speculating about how to test a particular hypothesis, we are moving into phase two of a project, implementation. The project might, however, be written up and evaluated before implementation in the form of a Research Proposal. Often the basis of a Research Proposal is the kind of information found in the Introduction, Hypothesis, Methods, and Bibliography sections as we have studied them. Therefore, using all of the exercises and analysis we have reviewed in this text, you should now be ready to write a Research Proposal about your own area of interest, taking the form of Introduction, Hypothesis, Methods and Bibliography we have been discussing, about a project in a small area of the social sciences which would corroborate or correct previous research in some fashion.

CHAPTER IV - FROM METHODS' TO CONCLUSION
(THE SOCIAL SCIENCES)

"I am tired of term papers. I would like to try real research."

The student who spoke these words meant he was tired of starting and ending his papers in the library, and felt that there must be more to research than that. Our study of academic research so far shows us that he is partly right. Two of the sources of research are the genuine fascination with aspects of the real world and the desire to get close to, to understand, to know in depth, that part of the real world. Research is an active engagement with the things of this world. If a third source of that research is found in the library it is to be used as a context for our own research activities.

With this in mind you should be ready to use the thinking, writing and library activities generated by the last three chapters to help you continue with your research proposal of a test to corroborate the findings of others. Since we have based this "derivative study" in the social science area, the activities of such research can and often do take place in the many environments of the college campus, from cafeterias, to classrooms, to fraternity houses. It is true that as a beginner you may not have the knowledge of social science to help you interpret your data, nevertheless, there is much in a social science experiment that is quite accessible and always interesting. In order to take full advantage of this project we will review the Methods, Results and Discussion sections of a project and then urge you to get going with your own data gathering.

Social Science Methods

You already know that the Methods section describes how the hypothesis is to be tested, and that there must be a tight relationship between these two aspects of your project. In the research proposal you have written you may have restated the methodology found in your preliminary reading or you may have formulated your own. This is the time, however, to evaluate thoroughly what method you will use to test your hypothesis. The second half of this chapter will provide a list of steps that you may take to implement your methodology. Right now consider that the methodology suggested by your reading may be unsuitable; it may call for tests not accessible to you, or depend on places you may not be able to visit or use, or provide data that you are not prepared to interpret. What we are looking for is some way for you to isolate an aspect of human experience through methods you can realistically try so that you may understand an element of human behavior, such as motives, growth patterns or group dynamics. In order to find an appropriate method, let us first review some concerns special to the social scientist.

The social scientist tries to measure what may seem unmeasurable. The social scientist does this by limiting exactly what behavior is studied and by objectifying the experience. One way for us to limit human experience is to choose a general approach to the area under study. For example, if alcoholism is under study, then are we interested in knowing about individuals' behavior (psychology) or about group behavior (sociology)?; if peer pressure is under study, then are we interested in knowing about our contemporaries (social psychology) or about other cultures (anthropology or comparative sociology)? We might follow up these early decisions by further limiting the behavioral focus. Do we want to know how particular individuals have become alcoholics or what are group attitudes towards drinking? Do we want to know if peer pressure motivates team players or how some other culture allows for individuality? Motives, attitudes, behavior--what do we want to know? About what individuals or groups? In what environment?

Once we have answered these questions we can turn to looking for a means of observing these aspects of human experience so that our observations are reliable and verifiable. If other social scientists repeat our observations about the experience, then they should be able to see or find the same data about the same behavior. Since the unique or "quirky" way of seeing is not of interest here (usually), most social scientists want to be able to generalize their observations in order to predict and understand human behavior. So the social scientist tries to measure behavior objectively, experimenting or observing in a way that the data emerges from the subject(s) rather than from the bias of the observer. The social scientist has developed many ways of observing while trying to remain objective. Here are four possible methods: 1) *Questionnaires and surveys* offer one way to ask large numbers of people exactly the same questions. They sometimes enable us to get at group attitudes and experiences, and they yield quantitative results. 2) *Interviews* can yield in depth information about personal experience and provide verbal and non-verbal clues to behavior. 3) *Observations,* either as an outsider or as someone participating in a group or activity, can yield insights into the dynamics of a situation, environment or group. They also can yield quantitative results. 4) *Case studies* call for us to gather as much information about an event as possible and to consider all available data, providing a multi-faceted picture of human experience.

Each of these methods may be used to explore human behavior, but each will yield different data and lead to different insights. A questionnaire about drinking will yield different insights than a series of interviews. Before choosing a particular methodology with which to test your hypothesis consider very specifically what each method will yield in data and in possible insights.

Exercise
1. Fill out the chart at the end of this text entitled "Chapter IV: Exploring Choices in Methodologies," drawing upon the discussion above as necessary.
2. Reviewing the chart, select the best methodology and revise your Methodology section from your Research Proposal as necessary.

Limitations of Each Method

No one method measures all aspects of human experience, nor does any one method yield clearer data than another. The chart just completed in the exercise above shows that we can choose among these methods of the social scientist, matching them most appropriately to the aims we have set upon our study. Interviews, for example, might be most suitable if we are interested in individual motivations, while questionnaires might be more suitable if we wish to measure group attitudes. Of course, it is wise also to consider the limitations intrinsic to each method before making a final choice. The Application section of this chapter explores some of these limitations in detail, but at this point a few general statements will help you choose an appropriate method for your project.

Questionnaires are only as good as the questions, and do not allow for the researcher to follow up important responses with more probing questions. In addition, questionnaires might call for a population that we do not have time nor access to select or administer. Interviews depend upon the skill with which the researcher can elicit responses without prejudicing the answers. It is one thing to ask, for example, "who will you vote for?" and quite another to ask, "You are voting for Ray Smith, the best man for the job, aren't you?" The interviewer also has to decide how responses will be recorded so as not to interfere with the interview.

48

Interviewing may take some practice to do well. Observations frequently offer problems in terms of the speed, thoroughness and accuracy with which they sometimes must be recorded. I have seen instances where the behavior is over before the observer is able to record the response. Thus, choosing the behavior to observe is sometimes the most significant and problematic aspect of this method. Success, however, depends on the skill and objectivity of the observer. Finally, case studies often call for a length of time and access to data which the beginner may not be able to manage. Even though each approach has its limitations, one will seem more suitable than the others for eliciting and measuring the behavior you are studying, and this will be your choice.

Exercise
1. Add a column to your chart of the previous exercise which explains the limitations of each method for your particular subject.

Interpreting the Findings of the Methodology

Once you have chosen your methodology and followed through by gathering the data, you will be faced with two creative tasks: *organizing the results and discussing their meaning.* In their crudest forms, the data you have gathered are merely numbers or answers or observations, not in themselves meaningful. The researcher tries to find the meaning in the data by organizing them to reveal patterns, highs, lows, quirks or notable responses. This is one way to reveal meaning. Another is to take these insights and tie them in with others' research experiences. Since both activities yield insights, both activities are presented in the written version of your research, the paper. In many published articles the Results, Discussion and Conclusions are often blended into one or two sections, but by dealing with these as discrete sections, we can appreciate the important aspects of each.

Results

In the social sciences as in the physical sciences, where observation and measurement are so crucial to the outcome, the Results, the data gathered, are frequently presented separately and neutrally, with numbers and records presented both in graphic and verbal displays. For example, observations of team members' behavior before a game might be presented in a chart with columns devoted to time and duration of observation, numbers of behavior observed, types of behaviors, and any other relevant, measurable variable, such as location or team standing etc. This information will also be reviewed verbally, in sentences and paragraphs which explain the table or graph, telling the reader what results to focus on, how to read the information. By presenting the findings graphically and verbally, the researcher is letting the reader see some of the raw data and is also explaining how the data has been treated so that their meanings are revealed.

Professional researchers often use mathematics, statistics and other kinds of analyses to find the meaning in data by looking for patterns, trends, relationships and the unusual. If the data are numerical, orderly arrangement usually is enough to show if there is an increase, a decrease, or no change; numbers plotted on graphs, with the average slope evenly crudely estimated can similarly reveal direction or trend. Another extremely important task made accessible by tables and graphs is to compare columns, clusters of data, and the concurrent direction of numbers. Social scientists are particularly interested in noting the relationships between two (or more) trends and directions (measured in sets of numbers). They call this relationship a correlation and follow statistical procedures to measure the correlation, called the correlation coefficient-efficient. If two sets of data are moving upward or downward at the same time, it is called a positive correlation. (If I take in more calories and I gain weight, there is a positive correlation.) If one set of values moves up while the other moves down, it is called a negative correlation. (For example, if I smoke fewer cigarettes and my lung capacity increases, there is a negative correlation.) If the data do not seem to relate by directionality, there is no correlation, zero correlation. I assume that few of us as beginners have the capacity to use the statistics to measure the correlation, but we do have the capacity to look at the figures for possible trends and to compare trends for possible correlation.

Another aspect of treating results that often concerns social scientists is that the phenomena they are studying occur more than by mere chance and the probable pattern of human events. If, for example, thirty percent of the students entering State University from Farm Central High School flunk out during their freshman year, we might guess that the high school did not prepare its students. On the other hand, if we also know that thirty-two percent of all freshmen usually flunk out, then Farm Central does not look too bad. The thirty percent seems within the normal pattern. Even if in one year thirty-eight percent of Farm Central's freshmen flunk out, this might be a chance deviation from the norm. Statisticians have specific procedures for measuring probabilities, chance, and deviations (standard deviation) which are essential for understanding results, and in order to overcome the problems of chance variations they can statistically determine how large samples should be to provide meaningful data. Once again, we, as beginners, usually do not have the skills to perform these procedures. Nevertheless, we can be aware that some of the data we derive from questionnaires and surveys merely indicate trends and meaning. We can be tentative in suggesting absolute findings, we should question whether our results vary from normal random human variation and we should call for further statistical analysis if we suspect it is necessary. When we read the reports of professionals we can appreciate the necessity for statistical analysis and bring to it a rudimentary understanding.

If the results are primarily verbal and not to be quantified, the social scientist still strives to let the results speak for themselves by tying the interpretation of gathered statements to a narrow perspective provided by advanced, specialized training. From a Freudian perspective, for example, certain verbal statements gain extreme importance and reveal motives, pathology or growth and development. As beginners we most probably do not have this expertise, but we can try our hand at two interpretive tasks. First, we can decide how to handle and present the verbal data (whether gathered in writing or on tapes) without simply repeating transcripts of entire interviews. Second, we can look for what we think to be revealing statements, repeated processes, contradictory responses and important clusters of responses, and explain these insights in the best writing we can execute at this time.

Exercises
1. Add a column to your chart which speculates on the kind of data generated by your methodology and on how you might choose to treat this data.
2. Review a Results section of one of your readings. Write an entry in your journal which rewrites the results for a high school audience.

Discussion
Once the patterns are noted, and the data presented, the implications of these observations may be discussed in a separate section with the title "Discussion" (or a similar title word). As we learned from our science paper, it is here that 1) the important results are noted, 2) unusual findings explained, 3) the procedure is thoroughly reviewed and 4) the links to the findings of others might be considered.

It is here that you find out not just what happened, but why it happened and what it means. It is here, too, that you can gain insight into the field and the topic. By the time the Discussion is finished, you should be ready to evaluate whether or not your hypothesis has been supported, and what direction future research should follow. These insights form a fitting conclusion to any project.

Exercises
1. Write a journal entry which speculates how and where your findings will fit into other's findings.
2. Using one of your models, write a descriptive outline of the Discussion section.

Application

Using your bibliography skills, your ability to select and shape an hypothesis, and your choice of method based on the exercise chart, you should now be on the brink of designing your specific methodology, and then analyzing your results and writing up your Discussion and Conclusion.

Methods Design and Restrictions

In the discussion above we narrowed your choices of methodology to one of four approaches (interview, questionnaires, observations or case history). The design and implementation of each one presents a variety of challenges for you to meet before you can proceed with your project.

Interviews
If you have chosen to interview you must first prepare your questions, practice your technique, and target your population. Preparing questions, your first task, might seem a simple matter of listing the most pointed statements interrogatively, but each question should be evaluated against your hypothesis. The failure in this link is one of the most prominent failings in student generated research in the beginning. One student wanted to investigate the importance of personal mood vs. team pressure on the individual's performance during an event. But the questions he designed revealed only which sports has "team spirit." He forgot to ask questions about personal mood and performance. Since he did not discover this until he had finished his interviews, he invalidated half of his hypothesis. He could have avoided this error if he had looked at the wording of his hypothesis and made a preparatory list of questions, the sum of which addressed each issue of the hypothesis.

Another constraint upon selecting and writing questions is that direct questions sometimes do not elicit a pouring forth of honest information. The wording of questions cannot be considered too carefully. One student found that if she asked "Do you smoke marijuana?" she received few positive responses. If she asked "How many times a week do you smoke marijuana?" she received numerical answers that indicated marijuana use was widespread and frequent. You must work and rework the wording of your questions so as to pinpoint the information you wish to elicit. Perhaps the best advice here is to try out questions on some test respondents, and to have a professional review your wording.

Even with well written questions, honest responses might come only after you have gained the respect or trust of your respondent. This sense of communication must stay in place throughout the interview. Therefore, after you have carefully written your questions, make sure you are ready to present yourself in a comfortable and efficient manner. I have found it is sometimes best to strive for a conversational approach, letting some of the questions and answers lead where they may, rather than stick rigidly to a question sheet pinned to a clipboard. Weaving your carefully worded questions into a conversational mode of presentation may take some practice on your part before you are ready to proceed.

Once you feel confident as an interviewer, select a place that is comfortable for you and your respondent, allow enough time for good communication to develop, and, most of all, be ready to record answers in a way that does not interfere with the conversation. You will want to record the responses as accurately as possible, but you will not want to take dictation. Ideally, you should converse your way through the interview, and write down every word afterward, out of sight of the respondent. Since few of us have this skill of total recall, we must either take accurate notes or use a tape recorder or come up with another method. In any case make sure it does not intrude upon the interview. Once again, you should probably practice your technique before beginning your interviews.

With your questions in hand and your technique ready, you should choose your respondents. Once again, depend upon a well written hypothesis to limit the field. In the sports study mentioned above, the student interviewed any player he could locate, and wound up with much more data from players of individual events (like marathon runners) rather than team events (like basketball). Had he kept his hypothesis about team spirit in mind, he would have made better choices. A further guide to the population is to interview as many people as possible, noting your time constraints and, especially, the amount of data you will be able to handle. For example another student wanted to see if being a fan of popular music was a causal factor in poor relations between parent and adolescent, but too many interviews gave the student too much data and a tangle of possible causes. Had he limited his interviews to one family unit, he would have had plenty of material from a core of essential people.

Once you have questions, technique and respondents, you are ready to proceed.

Questionnaires

If you choose questionnaires, some of the same issues and some new ones must be confronted. As with interviews, choosing and writing the questions and choosing the population are very important. In addition, you should consider the design of the questionnaire and its administration.

All of the guidelines we discussed for choosing questions for interviews apply when choosing questions for questionnaires: matching to the hypothesis, careful wording and careful presentation. The extra care that must be taken with this format, however, comes from a problem intrinsic to the writing situation: once the questionnaire is in the hands of the subject, you cannot control the situation or the responses; the chances that the subject will misread, not follow directions, answer impetuously, or not take your project seriously are all too high. Only extremely well written questions will avoid these pitfalls. Take a lot of time to consider how the wording of each question will elicit each response. Test each question to judge if the language communicates your message, and leads easily to the responses listed on your questionnaire.

Questionnaires should have an advantage for the researcher in that they can be objective and comprehensive. This will be true, however, only if your design is effective. You must design a format that can be given to each respondent in the same manner, with clear or obvious instructions for the person asking questions and the respondent, insuring uniformity and repeated accuracy over a wide ranging population. Make any instructions absolutely clear and test them on new listeners to see if they are effective. Make sure that each questionnaire will be administered in a manner that is the same as each other one. One group of students decided to ask questions as a group. They listed their questions together, but never worked out the format, the instructions, or the procedure. When they met a week later with "results," each had such varied experiences and responses there was no basis for a pooling of information; they each had only bits and pieces. They should have aimed for a form that was well written from beginning to end, simple and portable, and easily reproducible.

If they had designed a form they would have solved the most frequent puzzles of questionnaire design. Some of the most frequent puzzles have to do with answer format, questions and testers. What about answers: should they be listed, as in a checkoff, or should they be open ended? Should they be written by the respondent or by the tester? What about questions: should they be oral or written? How many should be asked? What about the tester? Should he/she be the researcher or some neutral party? What about the questionnaire: How can you measure its effectiveness? Is there time for a trial run? How should it be distributed? These and many other problems must be solved as suits your subject matter before beginning the survey. As guidelines in solving them, remember you are aiming at a procedure that is 1) effective and uniform; one that 2) elicits important information quickly and easily; one that 3) minimizes environmental interference; and one that 4) elicits responses that are verifiable and may be repeated. Once designed, you should check the format with a social science professional.

If you have written your questions and instructions, designed a clear format, and decided how to distribute and administer the questionnaire, you should target your respondents. Unlike interviews, questionnaires offer the opportunity to gather responses from large groups of people. Social scientists are aware, however, that just picking people off the street in large numbers may not get at the population suitable for the questionnaire, so they have developed sampling techniques which assure that the respondents represent the kind of people aimed at in the study. As beginners we are not familiar with sampling, but we can try to characterize our typical respondents, consider carefully how and where they might be approached, and how to administer the questionnaire to as many as possible. If you take time to target your population, you may avoid a common limitation of these studies, inadequate or inappropriate samples.

Once you have tried out your questionnaire and format on a few of your respondents and you are satisfied that it is clear and generates the kind of data you want, then proceed with the test.

Observations

The third methodology you may choose, observation, introduces design tasks that are different from those we have already considered. Here you must isolate the very specific behavior, match it to the circumstance that will elicit the behavior, design the circumstance, and design the observer's activities.

When isolating the specific behavior you are interested in observing, you should remember the aid of the well written hypothesis, with its wording as the guide in narrowing the focus. In this instance, however, you might find yourself moving from a large label of behavior to the very specific manifestation. For example, if you are interested in "lying" behavior, what specific responses in time and space will show the appropriate responses? One group of researchers asked respondents to lie about pictures they were looking at while the observers watched the respondents. Another group of researchers deliberately gave the wrong change to "unaware" customers at a cash register, then closely observed those who did and did not return the extra money. Which team's design more effectively revealed lying behavior? This question can be answered by realizing that each design highlighted different aspects of the large behavior, "lying." The picture test highlighted some physical facial behaviors of lying, while the money test highlighted some decision making behaviors. Each test served the very narrow purposes of the researchers. The challenge for you in such test design is to find the specific circumstances which will highlight the exact behavior you wish to observe.

Test design can be a challenging and imaginative activity. We can take the opportunity to imagine a set of circumstances which actually highlights our

53

pinpointed behaviors, and then face the challenge of turning the imagined into a real situation. On the other hand, we can examine the flow of life to see if natural circumstances offer observations of isolated behaviors, or we can combine the artificial and natural, as in the money test. To get a sense of the range of possibilities, return to the methods sections of your readings and note the many possible designs. When reading, imagine the test played out before your eyes, noting how the designer is trying to control the test circumstances. Is there a controlled environment, one that the researcher has created and one that restrains outside interference? If not, what restraints of time, observations or environment has the designer built into his test so that the behavior can be highlighted? Even though we are not professionals, our reading offers us the opportunity to appreciate these test designs and decisions.

Our reading also offers the opportunity for imitation. Whenever possible, we should adopt or adapt a test designed by professionals. Since test design is usually intricately tied to social science expertise (and a knowledge of variables and how to control those variables), we assure ourselves of better data if we can use an established test. When imitating, do not hesitate to make changes where necessary. Work to simplify the test for your use, your environment, and your level of training. Do not doubt, however, that a beginner can improve upon test design. Even professionals sometimes blunder. In the money study described above the researchers failed to account for those who simply did not count their change. The oversight made the results seem foolish. Bring all your critical acumen and imagination into play in test design, but keep it simple, and you may be quite successful.

Whether you choose to create a test in an artificial setting or noiselessly intrude upon the real world, your aim will be to lay out a procedure that may be repeated, verifiable and objective. The best way to do this is to write out the procedure as well as the instructions for each person involved in the activity, even for those participants who may be unaware of the test; then analyze the descriptions to see if they are really possible. Is the test simple and does it fit comfortably into time and environmental restrictions? Will the subjects understand the instructions or remain unaware if necessary? Are the observers procedures absolutely clear?

Looking carefully at the observers' role often highlights any flaws in test design. It is the observers' job to recognize the desired behavior and to record the data accurately and, usually, unobtrusively. The observer may need practice in any one of these tasks, and should be provided with the opportunity under real test circumstances. In one situation observers were supposed to watch unaware participants in front of a college building, but when they got to the place they could not remain unnoticed. As a result, few of the participants were "unaware," and practically no good data were gathered. In another situation, where the observers were supposed to participate in a natural setting and also record data, the observers found that the behavior was over before they could make their entries. Once again, much of the data was simply useless. Careful instructions, trying out the procedure and designing a good data entry format would have avoided these problems.

Your design phase is not over until you have written your data entry format. Aim for a simple, uniform sheet that is easily reproducible. Match the behavior you are watching for with the simplest kind of record keeping format possible. A sheet that is easily reproduced, with regular columns for data entry makes the most sense. Whenever possible quantify the data entries or use a check-off system, and do not mix in personal responses of undifferentiated, generalized observations. ("He seemed upset"; "This must have hurt him.") This kind of observation yields non-objective, inaccurate data which may reveal more about the observer than the subject. Once again, practice any procedure involved, such as time or other measurements, especially if you intend to participate in the activity while you are making your observations. Remember that the goal is to minimize inaccuracy and subjectivity while still remaining a human observer.

The last step in test design, selection of the respondents, should follow all the precautions we have mentioned previously. Involving a few respondents in trial runs should help de-bug your test, and then you may proceed through as many trials as possible.

Case Study

This fourth choice of methodology, the multi-faceted study of one person or event or problem, actually combines many of the techniques we have just reviewed. Interviewing, written questions and observations may well be used in order to gather all available data. The researchers who choose this method may also find a need to analyze written documents and statistical evidence, or the need to keep a record of a sequence of events for later interpretation. The new skills related to case study might not be procedural as much as analytical and interpretive of the data. With this in mind, the approaches and materials discussed in Chapter V through VII, where document analysis is emphasized, may be helpful. For now it is necessary to be aware that case study used as a test of an hypothesis is usually appropriate only if the researcher can focus on one present circumstance or person, and manipulate the variable to actually perform a test. Usually only a professional has such an option.

Final Checks of Methodology

Although you may have more than enough instructions for methods design, there are a few over-all checks you must consider. These relate to each of the methods described. Have you chosen a population you can really contact? Do you have access to the correct area? Do you need permission from someone to do what you want to do where you want to do it? One class was happily taking a survey in front of a Student Union of a college campus when the Director came rushing out and threatened to arrest the instructor for soliciting without permission. Another student wanted to speak to track team members just before they practiced, only to find she did not have access to the men's locker room. Check out all the rules and regulations, and use common sense.

A last check is to be sure that whatever method you choose, it gives you the kind of data you can handle. Do you want verbal data and to interpret those kinds of responses or do you need quantitative data? Can you handle simple number analysis? Which data are better to test your hypothesis? If you feel secure in this area, proceed with your method.

Exercises
1. Choose a method and lay out the design by following the suggestions above.
2. Practice the procedure and redesign as necessary.
3. Write your Methods section, and share it with the class.
4. Implement your methodology.

Results

When we turn to our gathered data, our results, we want to analyze them in an unprejudiced and open-minded fashion. We have already said we must let the results speak for themselves. The temptation is to impose our own wish of what the data should be upon what the data really indicates. One student tried to find out if choice of a style of clothing indicated taste preferences in other areas, such as music, television shows, and political candidates. When she looked at the results, she could not find any way to present the data, because she presumed they would show that all taste preferences are tied in with clothing fashion preferences. When we looked at the patterns without any assumptions we found that there was no relation between a fashion choice and the other preferences. The data seemed to disprove the hypothesis in this case, but the student could not see this until she let the results speak for themselves.

We have already discussed how professional researchers use mathematics, statistics and other kinds of analyses to find the meaning in data. We should try our hand at a rudimentary analysis by looking for patterns, trends, relationships and the unusual. If the data are numerical, then arrange them in tables or plot them on graphs. The numbers laid out in orderly arrangement usually is enough to show if there is an increase, a decrease, or no change; numbers plotted on graphs, with the average slope evenly crudely estimated can similarly reveal direction or trend. Compare columns, clusters of data, and the concurrent direction of numbers for possible trends and to compare trends for possible correlation. We are not expected to carry out statistical correlation procedure, but we can note the need for such analysis in our written texts.

We have also discussed how social scientists use statistics to overcome the problems of chance variations and sampling. Once again, we, as beginners, usually do not have the skills to perform these procedures. Nevertheless we can be aware that some of the data we derive from questionnaires and surveys merely indicate trends and meaning, and we should turn a critical eye to how the size and characteristics of our respondents might have limited the results of our study. We can be tentative in suggesting absolute findings, we should question whether our results vary from normal random human variation and we should call for further statistical analysis if we suspect it is necessary as we write up our results. Of course, any procedural quirks should receive the same attention in the written text.

If much of the data is verbal, your challenge will be how to present the material without repeating every word, and whether to mix in or separate your analysis from your data presentation. To some extent the answers may be found in evaluating the complexity of your data. If a lot of verbal data have been gathered, then presenting them in clusters with immediate analysis may make them more clear. If the total data may be clearly presented as a whole unit, then analyzed without much repetition, this method is preferable. Evaluate the data first, then choose the presentation. Either way, the analysis should point out what you think to be revealing statements, repeated responses, contradictory responses and important clusters of responses, and explain these insights in the best writing style you can execute at this time.

Exercises
1. Evaluate the nature of your data and plan its presentation.
2. Write the Results section of your paper and share it with your class.

Discussion

The final task of extracting meaning from data, the theme of the Discussion, is to tie our results and interpretations to other information. Since we have already listed four of the areas to be discussed, only a few helpful hints need be added. First, when comparing your findings with others', take note of the writing style which professionals use to make these comparisons. Note how discursive or brief these comparisons are, in what manner the reference is documented in the text, and how thorough, generally, is the review of outside literature. Secondly, in tying your interpretation or your results to any sort of generalized statement, theory or conclusion, be cautious in your wording and honest about the magnitude of your own limited project. Finally, extend this sense of honesty to a critique of your own project. By the time you reach the Discussion phase of your project, you will be quite aware of the limitations you have had to accept. Since these limit the meanings of your results, they should be acknowledged, although they may be tied in with a call for more research that solves some of the problems you encountered.

Laying out your project in this step-like fashion makes this kind of research seem very tied to a formula and almost inconsequential. In fact the efforts of the scientific method are aimed at controlling the experimental situation as much as possible and minimizing random or arbitrary events. Nevertheless, when researchers are at work on a project they may mentally move from step to step quite freely, such as reflecting upon their methods as they analyze results or gaining theoretical insights while carrying out methodology. We know from personal records of research that much critical insight about a problem comes during relaxation time. James D. Watson wrote that while searching for the structure of DNA he often went to the movies, almost hoping for a burst of insight while relaxing. Since you, as a beginner, must be very careful and self conscious as you proceed with your project, you should also provide time for free reflection and open ended thought about our project. The research journal you have begun during the hypothesis and bibliography stage should serve your purposes well here, letting you roam freely over the experiences, the insights, the boredom, the relevant and the irrelevant, as you proceed through your research.

By the time you have finished your treatment of the data and reflected upon the results, it will be an easy affair to judge whether or not your hypothesis has been supported and to explain briefly why. When you are ready to make these statements, it is time to write the Conclusion. The temptation at the end of such a study and paper is to want to make some sweeping statement about the importance of your subject and/or findings. Generally speaking, this type of paper refrains from making such statements. (In fact, some researchers stylistically understate the value of their projects in writing for professional journals; Crick and Watson said that the structure of DNA was of interest to biology, whereas their discovery revolutionized genetics.) As a matter of fact, the readers of your paper already understand the significance of the subject; they are more interested in the soundness of your methods and the interpretation of your results. The conclusion is brief and to the point; stylistically it is an understatement of all the effort you may have expended so far. A professional reader, however, will appreciate that the conclusion is merely one step in the research process.

Exercise
1. Write the Discussion and Conclusion sections of your paper.
2. Share these sections with the class.

Finishing the Project

As with every writing project, rewriting and editing are the final concerns of anyone who wants to communicate with others. The guidelines for review of a clear style, which we offered in the Preview sections, should be recalled and matched with a quick study of the style of your research models. Check to see if:

1. Your format is appropriate to your models.
2. The paragraphs are unified and coherent.
3. The paragraphs have the tension between general and specific as explained in Preview section 4.
4. The opening paragraphs contain the features listed in the Methodology of Chapter 1.

5. The Results and Discussion paragraphs follow the guidelines listed in this chapter.
6. The conclusion stays within the limits appropriate to the models.
7. The documentation is correct, to the finest detail, of the models.
8. The writing style, particularly word choice, is appropriate to the models.
9. The final copy is proofread.

Exercises
1. Rewrite the various sections of your paper to create a complete draft. Share it with members of your class, gathering comments from classmates and instructor. Revise, based on your evaluation and on your gathered comments.
2. Enter an extensive entry in your journal which reflects upon the experiences of this project. What was interesting, difficult, or new? What might you like to pursue? How has this effected your view of research and of writing? What other insights might you share with your classmates?

CHAPTER V - METHODOLOGY
IN LITERATURE AND THE ARTS

"What do scholars of literature do when they do their research?"
"I am not sure. Study the lives of authors?"

This is another snippet from a writing classroom conversation. When we turn from research in the sciences and social sciences to the humanities and the arts, there is general consternation about describing the methods of scholars in nonscientific fields. This consternation is not limited to students. In my own interviews with professors of literature and history I have found a wide-spread reluctance or inability to discuss methodology. Some of these professors have maintained that one learns literary or historical research by doing it. Alert students have frequently responded to this with the insight that they cannot do it unless they are shown how.

This quandary does not exist for scientists because methodology is such a prominent part of their discipline. When the scientist writes a research report, the methodology is described and often set off with its own section heading. If the methodology accounts for some twist in the results, that factor is openly discussed in the Discussion or Conclusion section. Often choice of methodology becomes a hotly debated item among scientists engaged in research on a similar problem. During the race to establish the structure of DNA, Watson and Crick were criticized for their choice of model building as a research technique; they eventually won a Nobel Prize for their discovery, which was based on model building. Clearly, in science, science methodology is discussed, chosen and written up; it plays a prominent role in the discipline.

Not only does science write and talk about method, it is also true that the general principles of science lead directly to its methodology. For example, science takes as a general principle that the natural world is orderly and predictable, that the same causes will lead to the same results. (If two chemical elements are mixed in the same way, they will each time produce the same reaction and product.) The consequence of this principle is that the scientists immediately understand that the task must be to study phenomena to find the orderly, predictable result; they measure and lay out the sequence. It is, generally speaking, also a principle of science that natural phenomena have natural causes that can be understood by close up, objective observation even of minutest parts. Consequently, the method of observation is impersonal, controlled, made numerical or systematic, until each part measured yields up its natural principles. The theory and the practice make a tight fit.

Science theory and practice also are prominent because the broadest principles and methods stretch across disciplines, even to the social sciences. Thus, although a chemist cannot automatically start doing biophysics because there is specialized knowledge needed, the chemist can accept the biophysicist's methods and findings if they are based on good science. In fact, the chemist might very well check the veracity of chemical research by making sure it blends with biophysics, because both areas accept the same principles of natural law. Biochemistry has played an important role in some studies of human development and behavior only as long as the research has been willing to include man as a phenomenon of natural laws so that all aspects of human life are scientifically knowable and measurable and predictable. Indeed, we have gained great understanding of human life, even of emotions, creativity and individuality by the applications of science theory and methods to mankind. When academicians of human behavior do research, they do science.

It is easy to see that the study of literature and the arts does not proceed in the same way or from the same set of assumptions. A look at the writing of literary scholars shows that they tend to write in a different format from scholars. If you have written papers for English class, you know that they do not feature section markers or methods statements. They probably do not have hypotheses, but they might have "thesis" statements or sentences. Those sentences were the only overt reference to some very important activity that transpired throughout the drafting or note taking or writing phases of those projects. None of that activity was really measurable and, in some ways, it was unique to you. The papers, which were the product of that activity, focused upon result and discussion, and obscured method. Any reader is forced to pay attention to the subject and to your insights, but not to your method. This is typical of the products of literary scholars.

To a large extent, the methods of scholars in the humanities and the arts are obscured also because they are not as overtly active or group oriented as are the scientists. The literary scholar may work alone, using time by reading, ruminating, writing and revising in the quiet of office or library. The creative moments and methods are simply not visible and usually not done as part of a team. The methodology is unnoticed or in the doing of reading, writing and thinking.

As to the general principles of literary theory, there is not the kind of universal agreement on the largest issues that we find in science, nor is there always cross-curriculum acceptance of general ideas. It seems to me that literary theory is often in a phase of redefinition; it is not uncommon for one large bookcase at my local bookstore to be devoted to books which are debating literary theory. In addition, for the last 150 years, at least, the humanities and arts have been profoundly effected by science and science method, and history, if not other academic areas, is now in a reaction to that influence.

Where, then, does that leave you, a student who may be for the first time trying to understand and do research? It means that you have to make an extra effort to unearth what you might know about literary and art scholarship, to review what the professors say about their activities, themselves, and also to turn to our experiences with these professionals to see if that helps us understand the nature of this research.

I intend to concentrate the rest of this discussion upon literary analysis, but most of these insights can and should be applied to art, drama and music as well. All of us must acknowledge that we have taken classes of literature, and we have studied literary texts, albeit under the guidance of an instructor. Think about the activities of that class. The instructor might have lectured or encouraged discussion. There might have been an effort to recreate the times or ideas out of which the literature emerged. There might have been lengthy discussion about the life of the author, major events and individual characteristics. There might have been a survey of the best works of a particular author or the representative authors of a period. At some time there must also be attention to the literature, itself-- the poem, the short story, the novel, etc. Ultimately, the scholar of literature calls upon all of these approaches to understand the particular piece of literature. Whatever the focus of the inquiry or discussion, the insights will eventually turn in this direction, a piece of literature.

Sometimes students call this discussion about literature "just talking." The instructor may encourage this "talking" by asking students to draw on individual experience with which to explain the piece or to explain why a student has read the piece in a particular way. In other courses the instructor may encourage this talking by asking for insight into various aspects of the piece itself, about character or plot, etc. Either way, the instructor is asking for involvement with the literature, and then a reflective analysis of that involvement. That reflective involvement is an activity of literary research.

Why should a literary scholar be so concerned about one piece of literature? Or about an author? Or about how we read a piece of literature? One way to answer those questions (although not the only way to answer them) is to reflect upon the centrality of literature in human life. In its many forms, from fiction, to scripts, to librettos, to essays, literature touches upon our lives, contributes to the quality of our lives, sets free our imagination, and even reflects our lives back to us. From primitive man onward the story teller has played a central role among groups of people, preserving the past, inspiring great effort among peoples, helping to create identities, and exposing human frailty. For centuries history was expressed through narrative, a form of story telling. Consider *The Iliad, The Odyssey, The Canterbury Tales, Hamlet,* consider Homer, Chaucer, Shakespeare. In all ages some of the greatest minds of mankind have chosen to express themselves through literature, perhaps because its many forms are the most powerful means for these geniuses to express their insights. It goes without saying that these insights, given to us as the experiences of literature, are no less important or true than the laws of nature that are revealed through science. They are another way of seeing into and expressing life. (This is true, too, for all of the arts.) These pieces of literature have a way of pulling us into their grip so that by the end of the work we cheer the hero, weep at the loss of great fortune or are outraged at life's injustices. Through the seduction of literary genius we see newly into the nature of things.

One purpose of literary research, therefore, is not so different from one purpose of scientific research: new knowledge--about life, about man, about the phenomenon of literature itself. This last interest, the literature itself, calls our attention again, for this is the focus of much literary research. If a piece of literature is powerful enough to give shape to a hero for a whole group of people, then the researcher wants to know what is it about that heroic type that is so powerful, how is the power communicated, what particular genius, at what time gave shape to the hero? If the play brings audiences to tears or to gusty laughter, sometimes century after century, then researchers want to explore the language, the dramatic pacing, the timeless themes, the mind of the genius author, among other questions about the play itself. They want to know about all aspects of the literature.

In order to answer these and many other questions about literature, researchers take all kinds of approaches to edge their way towards understanding, and the results are often the "talking" we have already described as part of the literature classroom, where you are often asked to participate. It is possible for you to participate in this inquiry about literature in many ways, by bringing your own experience to the reading, by learning about the author, or about the times, or by becoming familiar with the elements of literature (such as character, plot, etc.). In your classroom I am sure that the last kind of inquiry, the one centered around the elements of literature, often dominates much discussion (and may be thoroughly enriched by information from other areas of inquiry). This is because the literary scholar has found that by identifying and studying elements of literature as each seems to play out in a piece (the imagery of a particular poem; the character of a particular play; the symbolism of a particular novel) much of the artistry, the creative genius, the enduring power of the piece becomes accessible. It leads to new knowledge in literature.

Luckily for us as beginners or novices, the methodology is not out of reach, as it may be with some other lines of inquiry. We may not have the time or the background to recreate an historical period and place the piece in this context, and we probably do not have the psychological acumen and raw materials to carry out an effective biographical study, but we can read and reread and contemplate a particular piece of literature. By use of our intuition, our experience and careful critical analysis, each of us can gain some insight into the dynamics of a piece of literature. The steps involved in that analysis will be reviewed in detail in the

Application section of this chapter; for now we can make a few important generalizations.

Critical analysis or what we earlier called reflective involvement begins almost non-critically, by allowing yourself to become involved in the reading, by being drawn in, fascinated, aroused, even angered or repulsed. That beginning should be enough to provoke questions, first perhaps about your response, then gradually more perceptive questions about the piece that provoked that response. In finding the answers to your questions, you turn separately to the piece, and to the element (one or more) that is most provocative. You might, then, observe how the author has handled that element throughout the piece, by observing language, repetition, intensity, climax, conflict or any other pattern you perceive. Finally, as you back away from the analysis of one part of the piece, you can begin to make inferences about the whole, broadening your perspective to theme, or artist's purpose, or the enduring messages and power of the literature. This four step methodology takes practice, but can yield great satisfaction to all readers of literature.

If we compare these steps with the types of writing appropriate to literary analysis, we gain many interesting insights. First, as we noted before, a good deal of the methodology behind the writing of the research is simply obscured. The literary scholar does not write up a methods section. Instead, there may be a thesis and there may be verbal cues about method sprinkled as key words throughout the essay rather than explained as a primary meaning in the text. (These are often words like "compare" or "contrast" or "classify," etc.). Second, the bulk of the paper written by the literary scholar is often devoted to the analysis of particular elements or parts of the piece of literature. The scholar may even retell the story, pointing to meanings along the way, or paraphrase a poem in the language of the essay. Third, there is plenty of room in the retelling of the story for personal insight, and the subjective, authorial voice. The literary scholars uses "I," shares personal reading and teaching experiences, and wants personal experience to lead to creative insight. Sometimes parts of a literary paper are highly anecdotal and personal. Fourth, the parts, once examined are not left for readers to extract their own significance; the literary scholar carefully directs the reader to see the significance of the analysis by viewing the whole in some way. The literary scholar is not afraid of generalizations, statements of significance or moral judgments. These are often found in the paper.

These insights (about the four-step method of literary analysis and the writing style of the literary scholar) serve to tie together some of the theory and practice of literary research. We may now see that a piece of literature may be understood by careful study of its parts. We see that the "study" proceeds in an organized, reflective, sometimes personal manner. We see that the style of the paper that is written by literary scholars reflects the subjective methods of literary research. Most importantly of all we see that by careful study and writing, literary research is another way to create knowledge, which is a major purpose of all of academic research.

Exercises
1. In your journal write an extensive entry which contrasts your methods in the social science paper with a possible approach in a literary paper on the same general topic.
2. Interview a professor in literature or the arts to find out what is being studied and how. Write a journal entry which compares your findings with the views presented in this chapter.
3. Read a movie or art review in a newspaper. Describe the methods of the critic and compare them to the discussion in this chapter.

As we turn now to putting these ideas into step by step practice, I suggest that we practice some of these techniques of study and writing before we encounter the writings of professionals, as we did with the scientific method. That way we may bring our new experience along as we join in the discussion of experts. Remember, too, that my remarks are pertinent to literature and the arts, even though the discussion may focus on literary texts.

First let us remind ourselves that the writing process, as well as research and writing, are recursive tasks, proceeding in a circle-like manner around a perimeter that encloses the activities of observation, thought, and putting words and sentences on a page. In our step-like review of literary analysis, I will explain some of the observation and thought aspects first and some of the writing aspects second, but you may find that in practice there is a good deal of overlap. Accordingly, I hope you turn to your journal throughout our practice of analysis and writing to keep track of thoughts that occur out of sequence.

Step 1

Our general discussion pointed out that analysis does not make sense if we are not already engaged in the piece in some way, even if that way is anger or puzzlement. After reading or viewing, you must immediately try to articulate your feelings and insights, even if they are as simple as, "There is something here that pleases me," or "There is something here that I do not understand." You must not, however, be content to let your instincts go unpursued. Start probing the piece to understand the dynamics of your response.

Exercises
1. Select a short piece of literature or interesting piece of art and get involved.
2. Pose a list of questions about the piece.

Step 2

The probe should begin by listing the parts of the whole that make up the piece we are exploring, and by trying to become familiar with how those parts function generally. For example, a short story; even though we may not be experts, we can name some of the parts that make up the whole. Most stories have a plot, characters, settings or scenes, time spans, special vocabulary that brings out imagery and symbolism, as well as other elements. Not all stories depend on all elements in the same way, but by examining some of these elements we may come to appreciate the dynamics of the story. For example, if a character has acted in a way that is puzzling, we might look closely at that character's nature, statements and thoughts, and activities to understand the action. If a story takes puzzling turns, we might look at the plot as it unfolds, noting where it gets complicated, tense, intense and resolved in order to understand why or how the author has dictated events in a particular way. Extend this method to the other elements you have named to 'get at' the piece.

Often, however, we must do more preparatory thought to make this approach helpful. We must reflect further on the ways in which the author might utilize each element in order to appreciate the decisions the author did make. For example, character: we have said we might get close to a character by noting his nature and so on. Well, it is rare that in fine literature that the author will label the nature of an important character. Even if the descriptive words are given, they are usually only partly true. Just as in life we do not often walk around saying "I am generous, noble, kind" (even if we believe ourselves so). How, then do we display our nature? Through action, words and deeds; through appearance and life style; through our interaction with others and their responses to us. The author, too, uses these devices to develop a character, especially a main character. So, in addition to what a character says about himself or herself, we must also note what actions are taken, what clothes are worn, what habits are followed, how other characters respond, and so on, until we think we have captured the nature of that character. Probably we might have to trace through the short story until we may deal with any change in words, thoughts, deed or actions, that may finally reveal our character's nature. In all of these ways and more an author may choose to render character, and if we are to study character, we must come to see this range of creative choice. Each element with which we want to deal, be it plot, imagery, symbol, etc., might call forth its own special appreciation and analysis before we can sense the dynamics of the whole piece.

The same procedure applies to music and the arts. After you are involved, remind yourself of all the elements at the artist's disposal (color, shape, line, perspective, etc.), and explore, within the limits of time and resources, how each element plays itself out within the whole. If you do not have enough experience or background to develop these lines of thought by yourself, draw on the expertise of others in your class, from your instructor, and from professionals in the field. Professionals might be very helpful additionally by helping you to isolate which element is most fruitful for your own study. If necessary dip briefly into introductory material suggested by a professional. Most of all, bring your own thoughts and experience to bear to help you learn more about each element.

Once you have decided what parts of the piece you will study intensively, take time to work through the whole piece and patiently explore all the suggestive avenues. If the piece is a story, work through from beginning to end; if a piece of music, listen sequentially and compare the various segments; if a piece of art, examine the elements within a schema, foreground-background, top-bottom, top layer-bottom layer, etc. to provide a structure for your inquiry. Be thorough and open minded, remain open to the suggestions of the piece. I have seen students end their detailed analysis after a few insights. This is a mistake, because not only do they miss appreciating most of the piece of literature, they are also left with little content for their papers. Do a full analysis.

Exercises
1. Choose the elements you will analyze and explain why.
2. Explain the ways those elements may be understood generally, and explain how these insights will help you to understand your piece.

Step 2 (continued)

Once you are prepared to follow your analytical approach, reread your piece slowly and in depth. Give yourself plenty of time to see how the author used the elements of literature to create the piece, particularly those you have chosen to study. As you proceed, *take notes,* recording your observations, adding your own commentary, and writing passages that may well end up as part of your paper. If your study is centered around character, for example, use your notes to make character sketches in your own words, describe a character's clothes, speech and actions in your own words, record other characters' responses to your character in your own words, and take note of change or growth. If your study traces imagery, observe the clusters of images chosen by the author, note the words chosen to describe these images, follow the images as they change or recur through the piece, and synchronize those changes with other elements of the piece. Whatever element you have chosen, work your insights through with ample reference to the story, but *in your own words*. The notes you take will be ready to use as a first draft of your paper, even though you are still engaged in analysis.

Exercises
1. Carry through your analysis in a series of notes.
2. Rewrite these notes to form one draft.

Step 3

The analysis stage will draw to a close once we sense that we are getting a feel for the whole. Sometimes this happens early in our study, and all the rest of the analysis will fall into place; sometimes this does not happen until writing a draft of the conclusion. Nevertheless, an understanding of the whole--the theme, or artistic purpose or method, or historic import, or other over-reaching insight--will tie the analysis together in a way that is satisfying to researcher and reader. The skill called upon here is the ability to generalize, to tie together particulars into a sensible whole. This activity of generalizing has the effect of adding import and significance to the analysis, but is usually a rather brief portion of the paper.

Exercises
1. Make some generalizations about your analysis and about your piece.
2. Write another draft of your analysis which makes room for your generalizations.

Step 4

As we move through the analysis of the particular, contemplate the whole, and gather our notes, we will gradually become concerned with the structure, format and style of the final paper. Much of what we have said earlier in this text applies here as well. We can gather a sense of the structure of the paper as soon as we are ready to lay out our notes in possible organizations, representing drafts of the body of the paper. Since the body of the paper presents the content of your analysis and demonstrates but does not state your methodology, you must use language carefully to "paste" the notes into a coherent, unified essay. As you present your analysis, use the transition passages and words to remind the reader of your key ideas and of the method. If you have compared characters, use the signal word "compare"; if you are explaining plot, use signal words like "next phase," "part number three . . ."; if you are exploring clusters of images, arrange and present them in groups, using signal words, "one type of image . . ." etc. Let the language demonstrate your method.

The body of the paper must be preceded by the introduction, and here you have the widest latitude so far any paper we have discussed. Rather than review research, which you may not yet even know, your task is simply to arouse the reader's interest in the literary problem and in the analysis to come. You do not have to preview the details of the analysis, and you may assume the reader knows the piece. You must simply involve the reader. Any writing strategy may be used, description, personal anecdote, questioning, presenting a problem, with the guideline that once the introduction is complete, the reader is ready to follow your analysis. Once again, a signal sentence, resembling an hypothesis is helpful. It should be a statement that presents both the main message and the organizing methodology. For example: "An analysis of character and language will solve the problem of the strange ending of this story." Here is another example: "If we compare the main character with others in the story, we can see how heroic he is." This two-pronged statement would give excellent focus to a paper.

Now that the introduction and body with matching hypothesis is drafted, it is time to consider the conclusion. It is usually in the conclusion that the broader aspects of the study are brought forward, because by that time the generalizations you have been working toward should make a good deal of sense. Once again, conclusions are not mere summary or restatement, nor are they an emotional gushing of approval of the greatness of the piece, but they are a chance to synthesize particular insights into a statement of significance. The body of the paper explored the truth of your analysis; the conclusion should explain why the subject is important.

Exercises
1. Reread your draft; write a good thesis and introduction.
2. Rewrite the body of the paper.

Step 4 (continued)

As you bring your paper towards its final version, remember that the methodology has been subjective, *your* interpretation, *your* reading, *your* questions. The paper is you. I am sure, therefore, you want to appear in your best light. Look closely at the way you have expressed yourself in this paper. Look at the language and sentences, not only for absolute correctness, but also for style. It is in this paper that you have a chance to choose strong verbs, and interesting but accurate adjectives. It is in this paper that you can share your insight through ample examples and elaborated ideas. It is in this paper that you can choose most freely how you want to be perceived by the reader. Make your revisions count.

Exercises
1. In the margins and between the lines of your text, rework the words, sentences and paragraphs.
2. Write a clean, finished draft of your paper.

Incorporating Outside Sources

After you have tried your mind and hand at this methodology, which is not complete until the paper is complete, it is time to return to the world of published scholarship. By starting at the beginning of the methodology again, by becoming involved in another piece, and then joining your analysis with the input of other thinkers, you will broaden your inquiry and deepen your reading or viewing experience. The outside research will help you at every step of the way. It will help you focus your questions onto currently important questions. It will provide more information for your analysis, including historical, biographical, creative and other perspectives. It will help you to induce the significance of your own analysis. It will suggest possibilities of writing styles which you may imitate, and guide you to a system of documentation. In all of these ways, the outside research will become a part of your method and your paper, integrating smoothly into the practiced structure, and allowing you, once again, to talk with experts.

CHAPTER VI - NOTE TAKING AND
THE REVIEW OF RESEARCH

When a class of students was asked if they would use note cards for library research if the instructor did not require them, only three students said yes. When the class was asked if they regularly xerox during library research instead of taking notes, almost every student said yes.

In the class in which this exchange occurred there was much laughing and whispering after each question. There were few students who would willingly choose the laborious task of thorough note taking from library reading unless they were policed by the instructor. These students seemed embarrassed by the little moment of truth revealed by the questions, but they need not have been, for most instructors and students have been tempted to lay out upon the desk the most relevant readings, pages open, passages highlighted, and simply begin writing. With the xerox machines scattered throughout the library, it is even more tempting than ever to work from original manuscripts into our own research paper. Who needs notes?

If the point of research is to copy other peoples' writing, then no one needs notes. It has been one of the major themes of this text, however, that research is much more than repeating the ideas of others. Throughout the last two chapters, as we have moved outward towards the community of experts, we have stressed that we are using--that is adapting, responding to, selecting from, and adding to--the ideas of others. Even in the introductions, when we must refer to the works of others, it is to create a context for our own subjects and to focus our own projects. So even when a simple, brief reference in the introduction appears to repeat the major idea of someone else's work, it is not copying, but the distillation of the writer's analysis of the original text as it is relevant to the writer's project.

It is true, however, that the short introductions and the limited bibliographic searches of the last few chapters have led us to the kind of paper in which extensive reading and analyses of others' works was not the focus, and note taking from documents may not have been too important. You may have sensed that this limited approach to the works of others distort the research process to some extent. We are now at the stage, however, when we can expand our contact with the ideas of others, make full use of the library's resources and try our hand at a very different kind of paper, a paper that is sometimes called a review of the research (although it serves a much wider purpose). This kind of paper requires extensive note taking, and is the kind of paper which, in professional research, often precedes the hypothesis testing and corroboration with which we are now familiar.

Defining the Review of Research

When we begin journal reading and encounter articles with titles such as, "Psychological Mood Stages in 'Average' Marathon Runners," we can easily feel adrift among the minutia of social science, without any sense of how to navigate our own project. In fact, we are right to feel this way; we should not set sail in any direction until we have a sense of the area. Professionals, too, usually take time to sort out an area before they design a specific project. One sociologist said that before he starts a project he has to get a sense of the field to know where it stands in practice and in theory. This search through the field often generates its own paper, the review of research, and/or, at the very least, a comprehensive bibliography of use to other professionals.

Before we review the features and structure of this paper, we should understand when this type of paper is important to the research community. We have just said that professionals often start with a review of research, but only sometimes does this result in a paper. If the field is moving clearly in a theoretical direction, if specific projects are corroborating and confirming findings, inching along in a few directions, then a review may not be important. But such research harmony does not last indefinitely. As more data accumulate, as projects proliferate, there again comes a need to sort out this plethora of information. New data often suggest new theoretical directions, previous hypotheses surface again, calling for new research, findings in related fields give a new directional shove to the main area of interest or simply a new way of seeing things, so groups of studies can be seen together, for the first time, by someone making a new chart of the sea of information. At any of these moments there is a sense that the field needs to be organized in order to be understood, that the links between practice and theory need to be sorted out and strengthened. This is when the review of research becomes important.

Seeing the Need for the Review of Research

For this kind of paper to succeed, there must be a need for someone to come in and organize things. There must be a need for someone to say these are the important ideas in the field at the moment, these are the important data, and these are the red herrings. This organizing vision is the creative genius of this kind of research. It can sniff out and state theory in a clear way, and it can evaluate findings for the large patterns they seem to indicate. When we finish a review of research, we should know where we are.

This need to organize and to make sense by classifying may spring from sources other than reading in research journals. There are many instances when the same method, organizing, is crucial to the research community. It exists when a plethora of information threatens to disrupt the norm of an area. For example, a few years ago in the field of composition many, many new texts appeared with new ways of teaching writing to college students. There were soon so many new texts that it became difficult for instructors to make quick choices of the best available texts, and the field appeared to be moving in many directions at once. In fact articles did appear which sorted out this information, and the publishers themselves started to provide new categories for writing texts. Reviews of research were plentiful. For another example we may turn to the field of music. For some time now compositions by Antonio Vivaldi (a seventeenth century Italian composer) which were lost have recently been found in Europe, so that by current estimates his output must have numbered in the hundreds of pieces. These finds may very well force a reconsideration of a composer who only recently seemed rather minor in the history of music; at the very least they will probably call for a musicologist to find a system of organizing those pieces into a sensible pattern, just as Mozart's and Bach's music has had to be sensibly organized by special classification systems.

In each of these cases there has been a need important to the knowledgeable research community to organize a newly chaotic situation. The system of organization which has solved the problem has arisen from the nature of the information itself. In these ways, this sort of paper starts, proceeds and looks very much like the review of research.

Special Insights of the Review of Research

The special kind of vision called upon by this paper is double vision; you must be able to examine the specific item and keep the general view in mind at the same time. You must be able to read and understand an article of research, let's say about marathoners and their good health, and then also understand and integrate another article about marathoners and obsessive behavior (and possibly ill mental health). In such cases it is not enough simply to repeat one researcher's findings and then another's. You must find and explain how both could possibly be true, while also explaining the kind of total and complex picture made of human experience by the diversity of academic research.

There are innumerable ways of accounting for diverse "facts," data, and explanations of researchers. First of all, the researchers, themselves, might start from different professional perspectives. In the marathon research just mentioned, one research team were professors of physical education and the other were psychologists. Not only did they start from the different perspectives of their specialties, but they used different measurements and, of course, arrived at different results. Even though they did not apparently agree about the health of marathon runners, they could both be right.

Often in the same field, however, there is often enough diversity of findings to keep a reviewer busy. In the case of a poem by Robert Frost, for example, there have been a range of interpretations that made lively debate for years. "Stopping By Woods On A Snowy Evening" was seen by some as praise to the quiet and restorative beauty of nature, and by others as expressing a death wish. The emotion with which both interpretations were put forth, as well as varying interpretations in between, makes an interesting history of how poetry may be read. Such diversity, however, does not prove that everyone is right in his own interpretation or that no interpretation is possible (as some students often claim about poetry). The challenge is to account for the diversity, and in this case it may have to do with the theory of poetry held by the interpreter--how poetry is written and how it should be read. Since most writers do not explain their theory before interpretation, the challenge of the reviewer of research is to add the perspective of theory in order to make sense of the interpretations.

Frost presents another interesting problem for a reviewer, for there are many impressions of him as a personality, and the alert researcher could find a diversity of portraits and feeling about Frost the man. To some he seemed to embody the crusty, proud, independent New England spirit, and to others he seemed much more mean spirited and self-serving. The contradictions abound, and in this case they seem to arise not only from the perspective of the viewer but from the sources as well, the raw materials, the memoirs, the interviews, the conversations, the events in his life, and of course, the poetry. For the total picture, the reviewer might have to start with a sophisticated theory of personality to allow for all the pieces of information to have their places.

Knowing the possible sources of chaos--the varying views of diverse professionals, the clash of theories within a profession or the mix of wide-ranging sources--helps in locating an interesting academic research problem and in finding solutions. In all of these situations we see a confusing or chaotic coming together of information, yielding an unclear picture. The creative researcher will evolve a clear picture by carefully accounting for and sorting out the information and laying lines of theory for possible explanation.

The Review of Research and Note Taking

All of these situations which call for a review of research also call for note taking that would be careful, thorough, most of all, analytical. Simply copying out information from any source would be a waste of time, postponing the inevitable need for analysis. The finished product must present the chaotic situation, thoroughly explain the sources of chaos, present a system for creating order, and perhaps point to future research. Somewhere between finding the original information and writing the final version you must find that system. The note taking step is the right time.

If we return to the picture of the class interview with which I opened this chapter, it should be clear that the class members viewed note taking simply as a step in transposing information from pages of books in the library to pages in the final paper. In that case, xeroxing and copying would be the quickest way to carry out that task. But in the kind of paper we are considering now, there are too many steps between the pages of books and the pages of the paper to make xeroxing an efficient step. Consider the steps you must take through this material: As you gather information you must start building a picture of each source, first on its own then as it seems to fit with other sources. You must sniff out the areas of agreement and disagreement and judge which seem to dominate. Then, if it is the case that chaos grows, at this moment you must begin to note the causes of confusion, which should help you to sniff out a system, a theory or several possible theories which might give some sort of order to the chaos. Whether you do this in the library as you go through the sources or at home in front of the xeroxed sheets, the steps must be taken.

There is another advantage to thorough note taking. If your encounters with sources are analytical from the very beginning, if they are characterized by questioning rather than repetition, then you are already writing your paper. The notes you produce if you read analytically will inevitably be immediately useful for your paper. Good notes, well taken, can even form the first draft of your paper. Would not this be a wonderful situation if, when you sit down late at night to work out your final version of your paper, you find you only have to lay your note cards out in a sensible order to have a draft of your paper? Then you could concentrate on the language and style of your final paper; you would have plenty of time for proofreading. For some of you this might be a new experience.

Getting Ready for the Project

If you are convinced or intrigued by this portrait of the writing-research process, then let it begin by arriving at the library prepared to be an effective note taker. This means arriving well equipped, having already decided how you will store your notes. Tearing out papers from a notebook is possible, and I see it often enough at the library, but I also see that professional researchers choose other means. They seem to choose well bound notebooks for observations and running, diary-like commentaries and notes (not mixing projects within a book). And for library work they choose note cards (even though no one polices them). Why? Barbara Tuchman, historian, says cards are portable, putting a clump in her purse so she always has them handy, and she also says they can be shuffled and reorganized as the writing proceeds. In other words, they uniquely serve several purposes of the researcher. I am tempted to add that their size forces us to do note taking rather than copying.

In review, then, we are embarking on a project which calls for another sort of research paper, a paper which focuses on gathering and analyzing outside sources and on note taking. With the help of your instructor you should select a subject area, in the humanities or social sciences, apply the steps you have practiced in the earlier chapters as they apply to this project and put special emphasis on the concepts and methods of this chapter to write your own review of research.

Exercises
1. Ask a professional in the humanities or social sciences for a model of a review of research. Write a descriptive outline of the model, and compare it to the description of a review of research as presented in this chapter.
2. Select a topic of interest to you, narrow the focus to an area of wide controversy or overfilled information, pose an organizing hypothesis, and do a brief bibliographical search to confirm your direction.

Application

So far we have discussed the need and aims of the review of research paper and the need for note cards. Now let us review some practical steps to take towards a finished project, starting with note taking.

Note Taking

As you embark upon your close exploration of the sources, you will already be supplied with the equipment you need to share your notes (cards etc.). In addition it is probably useful to have a standardized format in mind as you fill up each card, noting down the source title or author and page number on the same place on each card. Later, when you have collected many cards and start shifting them around for the writing phase, you will be glad to have noted essential information in the same spot. Some professionals also cross reference their note cards with their bibliography cards by use of a number code so that minimal documentation information need be copied on to the note card and yet no note card will be unidentified. In other words, an empty note card would first be labeled with the number of the source which matches up with a bibliography card number, then the only other entry before note taking need be the page number. Note taking can then proceed.

As you start your in depth reading, you will also start your review and evaluation of each source so that the notes you take will be maximally useful as soon as they are written. After you have briefly perused each source, you should ask yourself these and other questions:

1. What is the purpose of the reading? (Remember we have identified three purposes so far; you will find others.)
2. What is the hypothesis of this reading? In what context is the hypothesis presented?
3. What is the methodology?
4. In brief, what are the results, discussion, conclusion?
5. How relevant is this reading to my project?

By addressing the first four questions to the reading, we are following the kind of analysis suggested throughout this book. The fifth question will help you decide what kind of notes to take to make the wisest use of this reading for your paper.

Matching Notes to Needs

The logic of this method should be clear. If the reading is highly relevant to your project, you will need to take thorough notes. If it is somewhat relevant, your notes will not be thorough, but not sketchy either, and so on. Even if the reading turns out to be of little or no use, it is probably wise to note that on your card with the shortest summary, for research projects have a way of taking unexpected turns, calling for information that at first seemed irrelevant.

Some instructors of writing have given names to different kinds of notes (such as paraphrase, precis, summary and quote), but I think it is much more important to focus on the uses of the note and let that decision dictate how "in depth" your note will be.

Note Taking from an Important Source

Since most of us can quickly sense when a reading is central to our project, we can also quickly sense that we must record a lot of the information. This calls for a rendering of the original reading *in your own words*. If the information is important your goal is to keep the *message* in its original *order* and retain much of the *detail*. In order to avoid copying, however, you will use your own words. If you sense that you might need a particular passage in great depth as part of a discussion in your paper, then you might strive to preserve the length of the original. This might occur in the review of research paper, wherein the purpose is to present a critical overview of many pieces of research. The most important skill here is effective use of language to transpose the source material so that it is useful for your paper and is not simply a copy of the original.

This is the sort of note that will take the most time to write and calls for the most close examination of the text. You may work at a passage sentence by sentence, reproducing the meaning in language that is compatible with your paper. Sometimes it may even be necessary to keep the original meaning by keeping key words, marked off in quotes, within the text of your note, because the original word is well known or carries so much meaning. Interspersed through these transposed ideas you should insert two types of cue words that focus the passage for you: one set may be interpretive, such as "major point," "important idea," "new data"; the other set should be for documentation, such as "Smith finds . . .," "Jones goes on to say . . ." Such note taking is slow and arduous; is it worth it? The answer must be yes, if we remind ourselves that this sort of note taking style will probably become a large chunk of the final paper, and in its present form may constitute a first draft.

Notes from Relevant Sources

The kind of note just described may take time but will certainly not occur with each reading. Just as frequently, if not more so, you will probably judge a reading relevant, but need to utilize larger, less detailed chunks of information, particularly to blend together with other chunks of information in the review of research. Once again, you should strive to retain the original message and the order of ideas in your own words without much of the detail of the original. You might takes notes on whole passages or whole sections at once. Here, again, do not underestimate what you may need to remember when you are writing your paper. You should continue to intersperse your notes with references to the author's name ("As Smith says . . .") Although you may not devote a whole passage of discussion to a passage of the original, this sort of note lets you discuss the major points of the original. The skill needed here is the ability to condense without losing the force of the original.

Notes from Less Important Sources

Obviously as you move along there will be many sources which you will need to refer to only briefly and some only as part of a reference (especially in introductions). Clearly, then, a summary of large portions of the paper or even of the whole paper is certainly appropriate. The skill needed here is distillation, retaining only the original message. There is little temptation to copy here, but remember to add your own insight about the work and its value for your project.

Direct Quotation

During any of these note taking chores, it is always a temptation to quote extensively, particularly if you are taking notes in depth or if you like the way the original is written. Remember, however, that quotes in the final paper have great force if they are used sparingly and in strategic locations; then they add weight to our own writing. With this in mind, few quotes will have importance as notes. Long quoted passages and xeroxed passages remain as undigested material in the notes cards, eventually slowing down the writing process. At worst, these lead to intellectual dishonesty and plagiarism.

Notes from You as the Source

In order to enhance your note taking and streamline the writing phase there is another type of note card that ought to accompany notes from the source: notes about the notes. As you move from source to source you ought to pause to evaluate from special perspectives that will keep you from copying and provide further passages for your paper. These perspectives give you the kind of critical distance you need to prevent you from merely repeating others' ideas. For each important or relevant source ask the following:

1. What is the professional perspective of the author(s)? How does this show? Does it limit the study?
2. What seem to be the theories behind the paper (if you are able to make this judgment). Where do they show?
3. What sort of data or raw material is used? How is it analyzed? Are the data and discussion adequate?
4. How do the answers to #1,2,3 blend with the other sources? Where are the comparisons and contrasts?

Although answering these questions while you are taking notes adds an extra step to this process, it is certainly worth the extra effort and time for many reasons. First, it continues the critical perspective which should characterize all of your note taking. Second, you can answer these analytical questions while the reading is immediately in front of you, for easy reference and fresh insight. Third, the notes for these cards may provide the bulk of the content for your review of research paper; particularly if you give some thoughtful effort and provide examples from the reading transposed to your own words. For these and other reasons it behooves you to include these kinds of notes about each of the readings.

Note Taking and Your Journal

The kind of analytical-comparative thought that is prompted by the second group of questions will probably continue after you have left the library. If you are immersed in your project, if you are trying to figure out the research picture, if you are trying to organize the threads of information tangled around a subject, then it is unlikely that the only time you will think about the subject is in the library when you are reading an article. The problem solving, pattern seeking ruminations that are called forth at this stage tend to continue even when we are relaxing, and ideas tend to pop up even at unlikely moments. This calls for a third type of note taking--a return to our journals. At this point the journal can serve an important function by capturing brief insights, serving as a scratch pad for ideas half formed and for possible bits and snippets that might or might not become part of the final paper.

When note taking is complete, especially if all of these suggestions have been followed, you will have three kinds of notes, one explaining the content of the sources, one explaining the over all pattern or picture the sources create, and one that is a record of your insights as you have become more and more familiar with the material.

Exercises
1. Return to your bibliographic search and locate three types of sources: important, relevant and less important. Practice the notes important for each source, following the guidelines discussed in this chapter.
2. For each source, write note cards of analysis, as described in this chapter.
3. After you have tried your hand at all of the notes discussed in this chapter, write a journal entry which draws together the review of research with your sources. Explain where the chaos of information is evident and speculate how you will organize and present a complete picture of research.
4. Complete your note taking for this project.

Writing the Review of Research

The Format
If these notes are combined with an eye towards format, you also have a draft of your paper. Let us remind ourselves of what this paper looks like. We have characterized this paper by giving it many tasks. We said it identifies an area of chaos about a subject, whether the uncertainty is generated by conflicting data or findings, a plethora of information or research projects, posing of conflicting theories, or other sources of uncertainty. We said the paper presents, reviews and analyzes the most important work to date about the subject, whether the emphasis be on new information, practical methodology, theoretical directions, or elsewhere. We said the paper sorts the chaos into manageable categories to create a current picture of the subject, whether the current picture leaves many questions unanswered or offers your individual opinion. We said that the paper may point the way to future research in the field and offer opinions about the most promising directions.

Of course, as you plan and write your paper, you should choose to emphasize one or more of these tasks, allowing one or two to be de-emphasized or eliminated. The choice should be dictated by what you judge to be the most active and/or confused area of research about the subject. You must decide if there are scads of projects that need to be sorted; raw material that needs attention; theories abounding; multiple perspectives, etc. You must decide if you can identify theory or point to future research or if you will eliminate these sections. Make these decisions by reviewing your note cards. Once these decisions are made you can decide the structure of the paper.

The paper should open by focusing immediately on the chaotic situation and/or upon the need for direction in an area of confusion. The length of the opening will vary, depending on the subject and on the style of the academic field (which we will review below). As with earlier papers, the end of the introduction is often signaled by a statement of hypothesis, even though the sections will not be set apart or labeled. The hypothesis may be the kind of statement that carries two messages, your central message about the subject ("The many projects make a unified picture . . ." "The new data set the field in new directions . . ."), and your method of sorting out the chaos (". . . if we see the three groups of research;" ". . . if we see how the dominant theories are dictating research.") Obviously, you can not even begin to write your hypothesis unless you have digested your notes, made the decisions listed above, and decided what the paper will emphasize and in what order, but once you have written these opening parts, you have gone a long way towards controlling the

74

content of the rest of the paper. You probably now can lay out your note cards and have a rough read through of your paper.

Exercises
1. Write a journal entry, drawn from the above discussion, which describes the tasks you have chosen for your paper.
2. Write a draft of your introduction and a two pronged thesis statement.

The Classifying System

Another very important decision must now be made. How will you sort out the chaos? What is the organizing vision? Part of the organizing factor may come from identifying the source of the chaos, as we discussed in the first part of the chapter: perspectives, theories, data, sources, etc. If we can label and explain the source of the chaos, this is sometimes sufficient to bring order. At this point you should put this insight into a sentence. ("By reviewing the perspectives brought to the subject we can see the directions of research . . ." "The confusion comes from thirty recent experiments . . .") Sometimes, however, we also have to establish categories, classify, to create order. It might be exceedingly helpful to number the categories ("There are three perspectives . . .," "Within the thirty experiments there are ten that measure . . ."), or to assign names to categories ("There are Freudians, Marxists, and New Critics . . ."), or to divide by activity ("There are those who theorize and those who experiment . . ."), or find another way to classify. In each case you must be sure the groupings reflect characteristics that genuinely separate one cluster from another, and that the groupings create order. (It may be that every researcher is a theorist and performs experiments, so such groups do not make real clusters. It may also be that even though there are Freudians and Marxists, their interpretations do not explain the data, so the groups do not dispel the chaos.) If your groupings do bring insight to the confusion, then you should be able to stack up your note cards according to the categories you create, and you should have plenty of material to review in each category as you review the important points or describe information.

Once these decisions are made about emphasis and classifying vision, you should incorporate these into the structure of the paper by taking the following steps. First, lay out your note cards in various ways until you are satisfied that the flow of information matches a good system. Second, refine and rewrite the hypothesis so that it explains the system and predicts the flow of information. Third, write an outline or a series of topic sentences suggested by the note cards for the entire paper.

Exercises
1. Review and evaluate your hypothesis for the clarity with which it organizes and predicts the paper. Then underline the key words (those words which should be repeated throughout the paper to maintain unity and coherence.)
2. Review and evaluate your outline or topic sentences to see if they repeat the key words and maintain a flow of content.

The Body of the Paper

The body of the paper may now be devoted to your exploration of your categories. Here is where you will use your note cards, liberally drawing from them because they represent well thought out material. The cards provide the detail you need to show the reader the unique aspects of each category, your task being to explain part by part the qualities, the characteristics, or the data of each. You may need to describe, explain, define terms, lay out sequences, or use another pattern of elaboration. Once you have found a good way to set forth your information, it is helpful to the reader if you stay with the same or similar pattern of elaboration for each group you describe. (If you explain one perspective via its hypotheses and methods, then the other groups should be viewed in the same light. If you explain one source by matching it to a general category, then the other sources should be matched to their theories. Etc.) Since this is the body of the paper, do not under explain.

Another important task that accompanies this phase of the writing is to consider the stylistic preferences of your academic field. We have already discussed how to practice in text documentation and correct bibliography format. It is wise to take time to make sure you are using the right style in these areas by seeking a few samples from the readings.

We should now turn our attention to other stylistic concerns. In the previous papers we have emphasized that concise and accurate writing of processes and interpretation were demanded. We have also depended upon section markers (such as "Results") to hold the text together. It may well be that the academic field for which you are now writing expects a different approach. In addition to replacing section markers with explanatory language and passages, there may be room for much more development of ideas. There may be room for you to explain how you personally became involved with the subject or for you to describe your personal response to various sources. There may be more emphasis on the coherence and unity of the paper, and there may be room for you to rewrite to make the language more intense, perhaps more colorful, without distorting meaning. Look at your sources; what seems to be demanded stylistically of the authors? What latitude is there for the personal element? What type of language seems appropriate? Since the note cards provide content you should have plenty of time to revise and perfect the style of this paper.

When you have finished presenting your categories, and completed the other tasks you have chosen for your paper, you should consider the conclusion. Many students are tempted merely to summarize in the conclusion, but it is doubtful that such a review of the contents is necessary. Professional readers are probably much more interested in what research directions emerge from such a review of research. They want to know, also, what unanswered questions remain about the subject, what future theoretical picture seems to be forming, what are the area's debates? That is why the conclusions to these papers usually address the immediate future by answering these questions.

It goes without saying that you should give yourself time to revise your paper. Go about the revision process in three steps. First, check the paper for the qualities of good writing listed in the Preview sections: unity, coherence, paragraph development, sentencing and word choice. Second, match the format, style and documentation to your model. Third, carefully proofread.

Exercises
1. Write a journal entry which describes the format, style and documentation of your model.
2. Write a draft of the body and conclusion of your paper, based on suggestions in this chapter, and making them appropriate to your introduction and your hypothesis.
3. Review the analysis of your model and the steps of revision just discussed. Revise your paper as necessary.

An Overview

Once you have finished the review of research, you should feel that you understand the cutting edge of your subject, and are ready to talk to an expert as an expert. You will have located an area of your subject which is still under examination. You will have reviewed and organized the current direction of the field. You may have pointed to the future or you may have explained why the present is stymied. You will have produced a well written paper. The review of research is quite an achievement.

Exercises
1. Complete a final version of your paper.
2. Proofread for a professional looking manuscript.
3. Write an extensive journal entry which describes your new knowledge and your opinion of the review of research.

CHAPTER VII - METHODOLOGY AND
APPLYING A THEORY IN HISTORY

"What is it historians do when they do research?"
"They look at past events."

Once again, we start with a classroom discussion. This time my class was discussing the research activities of their history professors, and many students agreed that these scholars must be busy trying to find out what happened in the past. How can they find out what happened? Some students suggested that historians examine remnants of the past, such as unearthed pottery. A long silence followed.

Each student sensed that scholars who study the past must do much more than they had described, but when put on the spot, they were at a loss to describe that activity. Once again, we turned to the experience we have all shared, history class, with its lectures, tests and papers. Viewed from this angle, historians seem concerned with tracing events of the past, recreating a sequence of events, one leading to the other, until the semester is over or until the narrative leads to recent times (at which time political science and sociology seem to take over). My students reminded me, at this point, that the tests they had taken and the papers they had written had often been concerned not only with sequence but with causes, why one event leads to another and how many events seem to cause a major event, such as a war or the end of an era. Finally, a few students drew on their reading experience to remind us that sometimes historians are involved with describing the times, recapturing chunks of the past, sometimes with a good deal of force and color (such as in a historical novel or in a recreated village). Historians, then, are involved in a variety of research about past events, including trying to know what events happened and when, in what order, and what the life must have been like at those times.

This does not, however, explain how historians do their research. Before we answer that question, let us remind ourselves why there is such ambiguity, the same kind of ambiguity we faced with discussing the activities of the literary researcher. In that case we found that the methodology is not a feature of the final product, the essay or paper. The same condition is true in history; the final paper does not usually lay out a statement of methodology, but the writing (its structure, language and content) implies or even stands for the method. This does not mean that there is no methodology. Rather it suggests that there are methods we have not yet practiced being used to create new knowledge.

The Activities of the Historian

Looking at the raw materials of the historian we can begin to edge closer to their research activities. Those raw materials tend to be documents--yes, newspapers, but also government documents, letter, diaries, eye witness accounts, weather reports, literature, etc.--in short, anything that gives a clue to the event or times. But documents are only the beginning, for every artifact, from pottery, to buildings, to clothing, to food can be of historical value and yield new information (even though these are usually in the domain of related studies, such as art history, archeology, etc.). As they work away at their task, historians are confronted with the minutia, small and large, of past events.

Once confronted with the raw material, the historians must do something with it in order to find the spirit of the times and the sequence of events. If not dealt with, the collection of raw material would resemble an attic with junk strewn about under cobwebs, not making any sense, not even appealing for an hour's browsing, discouraging even to the cleaning lady. Once, again, some method of organizing is needed to establish order and significance. We have encountered this before in our discussions about research, and we turned to analysis and classification as helpful activities. At this stage, these activities are helpful to the historian as well. Just as we have practiced analyzing a literary piece for what it can tell us by studying its parts so, too, does each document of history need to be analyzed for what it yields to the historian. Just as we have found pattern by gathering and grouping, so, too, does the historian, looking for evidence of links between documents that serve to extend all the details known about an event, until the full picture is drawn.

Historian Barbara Tuchman, although not primarily an academic, is exceedingly articulate about these first steps, collecting raw material and reading each analytically. She emphasizes that she uses every scrap of primary material that she can find, memoirs, letters, diaries, etc. published and unpublished. With each she carefully combs the source for the detail which helps reconstruct an event. It is, she writes, "The very process of transforming a collection of personalities, dates, gun calipers, letters, and speeches into a narrative. . ." As she moves from source to source, Tuchman says she looks for corroborative detail, those bits of concrete information which confirm the truth of information from another source. If an eyewitness account reveals that the weather was overcast, Tuchman says she will check for an available weather report. If an historical figure was supposed to be tall, she looks for concrete details in clothing, furniture or house design to confirm the stature. The search for corroborative detail, Tuchman says, "is the excitement, the built-in treasure hunt, of writing history." Not only does corroborative detail help the historian deal with prejudiced primary sources, but it helps create a pattern through repetition until the full picture is clear.

Analysis, grouping, repetition, and the accumulation of data are all techniques we have already encountered and practice. In fact, these techniques sound very much like a blend of the sciences and the humanities methodologies we have studied. When possible, many historians try to lean towards the scientific when dealing with raw material, by being impartial when dealing with documents and by turning to quantitative data whenever possible (i.e. demographic studies). By impartially bringing together such detail, by selecting the significant through corroboration and impartial analysis, the historian often emerges not only with a picture of past events, but with a sequence of past events.

Some historians also claim the "science" of history is matched by its "art." These historians point out that insights about the historical significance of people, places and events occur to historians during close up, private study, after much private contemplation and individual rumination over the available evidence. (Tuchman adds a measure of "common sense" to the mix of the historian's recipe.) This is the very approach we described in Chapter V on literary analysis. Perhaps the historian's method requires a blend of "science" and "art;" The objective and the subjective; the public methods of science and the private approach of literature.

Special Problems of Causality

In doing history, the historian often wants to create a sequence of events. "Sequence," is one inevitable product of historical studies. Sequence creates order among millions of episodes, but it also brings us face to face with the problem of causality. Sequence implies that one event has led to the next event or has caused the next event. When we first looked at causality, or the ways in which we can know that if something happens another something will follow, we found a complex of problems which tested the methodologies of each academic area. The sciences have approached the problems through careful experimental controls and through impartial measurement of the natural environment. In the social sciences, the scientific method has proved helpful in studying the causes of human behavior, but the infinite varieties of the human environment and the difficulty of experimental controls have meant that many social scientists must include probability and sampling statistics in order to approach with any assurance that a cause has been identified. In the humanities, however, we have no sure way of quantifying causes.

Causality in the humanities is sometimes a matter of imagination, theory or intuitive guess. I say this not pejoratively, but with an eye towards our ability to measure human causes. This is why biographical studies often yield less insight into a piece of literature or art than does straight forward analysis of the piece itself. Who can prove that Beethoven's deafness led to a great, urgent outpouring of music, or that Van Gogh's approaching madness accounts for his intense, expressionist style? Most of the time, when we leap towards sequence of causality in affairs not before our eyes, the sequence is based on experience, common sense, and most of all on theory. Our innate human need to see or ascribe to order in the events around us blends with or is reinforced by personal experience until we come to accept a theory that explains why things happen.

Sometimes this "theory" is based on simple observations and is really an operative generalization. For example, the mother who has several children notices that each of her children at the age of two has become negative, throws tantrums, and pushes her away. By the third child she looks at the angry two year old and says, "It's the terrible twos." The generalization explains the behavior, lifts it out of the unexplainable, puts it in a sequence of development, and gives it meaning. By the same token, the professional researcher of human development may make hundreds, even thousands, of observations of children's behavior at different stages, describe them, and catalogue them, until they create a picture of "normal" development. (That professional may also say, "It's the terrible twos.") In fact this is just what researchers like A. L. Gesell and Jean Piaget did, and their work has allowed doctors, teachers and other professionals to carry around with them a "theory" of normal childhood development by which they can interpret the events, details and actions of each child they know.

Theory, however, is not a static entity. The very meaning of the word implies conjecture and the need to put the principles to the test. Other researchers of child development, for example, have built on Gesell's observations by viewing more, testing the principles, and by bringing to them other information, leading to the creation of much more comprehensive accounts of child development, and fully developed theory. In this way Piaget's theories, in particular, are exceedingly useful in explaining the full range of children's development, physical, emotional, creative and individual. Educators, and others, have found Piaget's ideas helpful and they apply his principles.

But they are still theory. As human experience continues and changes, and as our search for knowledge continues, the theory will grow, change or be replaced.

Similarly with history, we each carry with us generalizations about why events of the past have happened. Some of us who are articulate about these generalizations can consciously use them to explain the personal and historic events of our past. Those of us who have wide ranging education have been exposed to many theories of human behavior or history, and may ascribe to some with particular passion. In any event, we need this unified vision, this theory, to help us shape the sequence of events, to label the causes and the effects of history.

Applying a theory, then, is another way researchers carry on their investigations. In one sense, no research can go on without theory. (Even purely objective science rests on a theory of scientific philosophy and method). The anthropologist cannot observe primitive tribes without being equipped with a theory of groups and culture, otherwise every observed behavior will have the same meaning as every other behavior. The political scientist uses theories to explain the present and also to predict immediate developments. Based on the order the theory imposes on the present, the political scientist lays out the probable consequences of today's decisions or action for tomorrow. Applying a theory (consciously or unconsciously) completes the historian's methodology.

One way to appreciate this aspect of the historian's task is to bring the theory to the forefront of the research project. In literary studies this has often been done with interesting and even entertaining effect. Sir Lawrence Olivier's Freudian interpretation of Hamlet lent that character new life and dramatic depth. Historic events and politics, too, abound with material ripe for interpretation based on a particular theory of human behavior. Thomas Jefferson's statements about a theory of man informed and sparked the way we as a people have come to see our history, their relation to other countries and our future. In every area of human behavior there is opportunity to watch from a theoretical position.

It is now your task to explain an event or speculate about a current trend by using the conscious application of a theory. The second half of this chapter will help you make the decisions necessary to carry out your project.

Exercises
1. Write an entry in your journal which explains why applying a theory helps historians study past events.
2. Try to name three theories with which you are familiar and explain how to apply each of them to appropriate areas of behavior or events. Use the chart at the end of this text entitled, "Chapter VII: A Chart which Summarizes Three theories and their Applications" to complete this exercise.

Application

Getting Started

A first step in your application of a theory to find out about an event is much like the first step in previous projects, choose a subject, one of particular interest to you. In order to expand the subject matter and the availability of raw material, you might consider state or local historical events, neighborhood history, campus history or even family history. Another possible choice might be a contemporary event, but only if you think you might bring to it an unusual perspective and/or you might be able to make controlled first hand observations. (I think it is wise to exclude political developments from this exercise, because the tendency might be to turn the paper into argument rather than exploration.)

Next, as with earlier projects, start your investigation by using your journal to explore all you know about the event, retelling all the details with which you are familiar and about what aspects of the event you want to know more. Start asking questions, and make them more and more specific as you list them, touching upon the people, the times, the scene, or any other element that may seem important. Then turn your exploration to possible sources of information and raw data. If you have kept your event local, you might be able to get beyond newspapers to diaries, personal accounts, letters, and, in some cases, interviews. Review where information might be kept, whom you would have to speak to, what permissions you might need. As you work through these questions and lists, strive to narrow down the subject, close in on the time span, focus on a limited area and circle of people, and just what one or two questions about the event you might realistically be able to answer.

Exercises

1. Start your search for a subject by listing three other areas or events of local interest to you. Add a list of questions and sources about each.
2. Select the most promising area for your subject and fill in the chart at the end of this text entitled "Chapter VII: Subject-Analysis Chart to Begin a Project in History."

Finding a Theory

Another avenue you must begin to explore, almost as soon as you have chosen a subject, is the theoretical approach you will take. Now is the time to review college courses recently studied to find if you are already familiar with a theory which might shed some light on your event. In most cases you are looking for a perspective which explains group or individual behavior or which accounts for change by laying out the theoretical structure of causes and effects. Sometimes we have learned these theories through study of the writings of a major thinker, such as Darwin or Freud or Marx, and sometimes we have absorbed them as we have studied subject areas, such as sociology or art history. Do you think you can describe how a sociologist would approach a particular problem, for example? Laying out the sociological (or other) approach will bring you close to articulating theory. In this brief exploration you should again record as much as you know about the approach, and where and from whom might you quickly find out more. Most importantly, try to evaluate <u>if this theory or perspective will serve your purposes</u> as you try to find out about your event. If you are trying to find out about a campus sit-in of the sixties, would it help to use Piaget's theory of child development? Perhaps! On the other hand, you might bring more light to those events by choosing a theory that emphasizes group dynamics or sub-cultures, or one that is concerned specifically with political change.

If your knowledge of theory is shaky or nonexistent, at least brainstorm the various perspectives, perhaps by academic area, and then refine that list by selecting an approach which seems interesting and helpful. Encyclopedias, with their brief introductions and follow-up bibliographies, are an excellent place to seek initial direction. Once you have zeroed in on a perspective, seek help from experts in the field or by efficient background reading and introductions. Try to locate an introductory text to get a good overview. You will not become an expert overnight in a particular theory or approach, but you should be able to assemble major principles and to review established applications or a brief history of the theory itself. Move ahead from this point once you feel you know what kinds of questions can be answered by applying this theory.

Exercises

1. Choose an appropriate theory based on the above discussion and write a journal entry which briefly explains its history and/or principles. If you have written such an entry for an earlier exercise, add details here as may be helpful.
2. In as much detail as possible, speculate how the theory will help answer the questions listed on the chart at the end of this text entitled, "Chapter VII: Subject-Analysis Chart to Begin Applying a Theory in History."
3. Write a tentative thesis for the project which includes your narrow focus or question, and explains how your theory will supply a solution or organize new information to reveal an answer.

Gathering Materials

You may now be ready to start gathering and analyzing your materials, but here the step by step methodology becomes complicated. You may find yourself bouncing from task to task. You have started with questions about an event, and you have hypothesized that an approach will help you make sense out of the available information. But you also have an obligation to examine the materials critically and intelligently, without bending the apparent evidence. The theory should be helpful in providing a structure on which to hang events, but be wary that the evidence may not neatly fit into the theoretical structure; be prepared to deal with this with a critical eye towards the structure and the evidence.

To proceed in this difficult coming together of tasks, I would suggest that you focus at first upon the event and all the materials available to you about the event. Be imaginative about where you might find the materials. The local library will serve for events of local concern, but draw upon local institutions and people as well. Local newspapers keep all back editions; local historical societies and town halls have archives full of all kinds of interesting materials; local businesses and other organizations also keep their documents as records of their histories. Follow the search for sources through to local people who may have interesting information and documents of their own. Be persistent and be prepared to interview and read creatively.

Exercises

1. Locate several interesting sources.
2. Skim the materials in these sources; then adjust your focus, your questions and your theory so that you may do a thorough analysis of the information available in your sources.
3. Return to your tentative thesis written for an earlier exercise. Revise this sentence based on your preview of your sources.

Working with Sources

As you continue to gather and examine all the evidence available about the event, you should begin taking notes in the various ways practiced for earlier projects. Much of the evidence you deem as most important will tempt you to make wide use of xerox; remember, however, that extensive quoting distills the analytical effect of your paper. Take notes in your own words now, working through the analysis on the note cards, point by point as the theory dictates; it will be easy to attend to the writing later. If making observations is necessary, remember first to lay out an organized, efficient system of record keeping, based on information sought by the theory and enter the observations in a manner that will be readable long after the time of the observations. If you are conducting interviews, be ready to proceed in a manner that elicits and records information without interfering with the "conversation." Pursue the directions suggested by your theory, but do not let that cut off communication with your source. In every instance, it is your special challenge to balance the prejudices of your theory with the biases of the primary sources.

Next, using your best analytical techniques of texts, look at each document you find to see what information about events are suggested. As you move from document to document, the bits and pieces of information should start to create a complex picture, with each serving to confirm or undermine or ignore the evidence of the other. There are many ways to sort the material further, such as separating "facts" from "opinions," but I think the most fruitful aspects to keep track of are corroborative detail (which was discussed in the earlier part of this chapter) and who (or what) is the source of the information. Each piece of evidence or document represents an individual's perceptions, and carries with it its own slant. It is helpful in weighing the value of a piece of evidence if you can understand the slant. With each source, take time to give names, titles and relationships of the source to others involved in the event, to the event itself and to the larger events and community. While reviewing the source's information, evaluate the reliability of the source's perceptions, how close in time and space to the actual event, how involved in the event, when and how were the perceptions recorded, how conscious of an image or an impression was the recorder. (Recent historians of Custer's Last Stand have minimized the significance of Indian accounts of the event because they say the Indian witnesses had to give the impression of vulnerability to white investigators at the time.) There is no doubt that one individual's version might be full of "facts" that melt away to opinion when matched against another's version.

Secondary Sources

It may be, too, that your subject has been analyzed by others, be it contemporary commentators, historians shortly after event, or academicians who take up the research from the perspective of times past. In each case, you are dealing, of course, not with primary material, but with someone's interpretation of the evidence and the events, a secondary source. Secondary sources can be useful in many ways. They can guide you toward significant questions about the event, they can help narrow your focus, and they can point the way to important raw material. But they do not remove the necessity of analysis and interpretation; they add to it. When you add secondary sources to your research (and often it is a necessary starting point) you must find the slant behind that interpretation, too. Just as with the original sources, you should evaluate the secondary source writers for their relationships to the subject and events, to their audience, and to their scholarly or intellectual community. Evaluate, as well as you can, their coverage and analysis of primary sources, and identify their theoretical biases. All of this can become evidence in your own recounting of events.

Exercises
1. Take notes from your primary sources as follows:
   a. Note the source's version of events.
   b. Analyze the writer of the source, guided by our discussion.
   c. Speculate as to how the information from a. and b. above will blend with your questions and are shaped by our theory.
2. Take notes from your secondary sources, following steps a. and b. above, and add:
   d. Note how each secondary source adds to or narrows your focus.
   e. Identify from what theory each secondary source is working.

Using Your Theory

Most importantly of all, be ready to examine the evidence by applying the features of your theory. By being familiar with the parts of your theory, you may examine the sources in order to locate the significant details. Your theory, for example, may suggest that economic forces are at work when a significant change in human affairs occurs. It will be necessary for you to apply this principle when confronting your evidence, seeking out whatever economic information may be available. It is also your responsibility, however, not to strain or falsify the evidence to fit the theory. As with out other projects, we must acknowledge the limitations of our sources or our methods. Sometimes other sources or revision of theory emerges which supplies the necessary information or explains the missing links. (I had this experience while investigating one theory of writing by interviewing writers and following their writing process. One writer simply defied the pattern, his practice not fitting the theory. At the time I had to acknowledge the exception; today the theory has expanded to include the activities of this writer, too.)

Exercises

1. After note taking seems to be complete, write an outline of the parts of your theory which will serve to organize your notes.
2. Play with your note cards until they fit into an organization which is compatible with your theory.
3. Rewrite your tentative thesis to include the note card-theory relationship just established.

Your Journal

Since the process of applying a theory can sometimes be liberating in the insights it affords and sometimes constricting in the boundaries it sets, it is very important that you continue to use your journal to reflect upon the progress of your project. Use your journal to record any insights that may not get into your note cards, any questions that remain for you about the subject, the evidence, the theory, or the progress you are making with your project. It is often helpful, periodically, to take a view of the whole in your journal, just when you are buried in the details of your notes, or even to note favorite details when the writing is concerned with the sequence of events. The different perspective of the journal can be surprisingly useful.

Writing the Paper

First Decisions

As you finish your note taking phase and launch fully into writing, much the same concerns must be addressed as in the paper for Chapter V, with much of the same decisions to be made. Early on you should decide what latitude there is for the anecdotal, the descriptive and the personal; early on you should decide the method of in text and bibliographic citation; and early on you should decide if the rhetorical focus of the paper will be narrative or analytic (retelling the event or presenting an interpretation of the sources). Each of these decisions may be made with the advice of an instructor or by locating a few suitable models.

It is also helpful to block out the structure of your paper by laying out the note cards and choosing among possible patterns of organization. Remember, however, that you are seeking a structure that will feature the various principles you have applied to analyze the sources. It may be that you will need to include a section that explains the theory, followed by the narrative that demonstrates the principles; or it may be that the principles might be explained in the various parts of the paper as you review your sources or present your observations. Make the choices that will most easily dramatize your methodology, even though no section is labeled methodology.

The one sentence which should be formulated early and revised throughout the thinking and writing phases is the thesis sentence. In two previous papers we have practiced writing this one meaty sentence by including language which announces your content and your methodology. ("By using the framework of Piaget's theory of child

development, I can easily understand the campus riots of the late 1960's and '70's."
"The puzzling aspect of events in Newport during the 1820's are explained by the 'Scapegoat' theory of behavior.") Since a well shaped sentence serves to structure what must be analyzed, and, later on, what must be written, have a thesis lingering around the project all the time. You have started with a tentative thesis and reworked it as the project proceeded. Begin now to shape the final thesis. Often in this kind of project the final thesis will be written just when the final version of your paper is written.

Exercises
1. Locate a model for your paper. Write a journal entry which describes the model. Note the documentation style and other aspects of the writing which you will imitate.
2. Write a tentative outline of the content of your paper and a tentative descriptive outline.
3. Write a thesis suitable to your outline.
4. Write a draft of the body of your paper.

The Introduction and the Conclusion
You should also make your decisions concerning the various acceptable strategies of the introduction and the conclusion, as we reviewed them in Chapter VI. There we said that the opening should "hook" the reader, perhaps with a story or with a description (if the models allow for that), and should narrow into the two part focus of your paper; the puzzling event and the theory to be applied. There we said, too, that the conclusion will probably expand to point out the significance of your study, your subject or your theory. Since the introduction contains insights generated by the full discussion, it is usually wise not to write full introductions and conclusions until the body of the paper is well developed.

Exercises
1. Write a draft of the introduction and thesis. Write a draft of the conclusion.
2. Rewrite the body to create a unified and coherent paper.
3. Share your draft with your class.

Revision
If you have followed the suggestions of this chapter, you should have ample time to make rewriting the last step of this project. During the early drafts you have considered models which suggest appropriate form and style, you have practiced the ability to reproduce appropriate documentation, and you have derived a structure which reflects the methodology of applying a theory. During these last drafts take time to look at the writing, as we did with our very first paper. Listen to the sound of the words and sentences. Have you found the most precise words?; taken time to add color where possible?; looked at the sentence structure and breaks?; tested the paragraphs for unity, coherence, and tension between the general and the specific? If you have taken time to check each element (and to proofread) you should have a paper of which you are proud.

Exercises
1. Write a final version of your paper.
2. Write an extensive journal entry which records your new knowledge and your opinion of this project.

Final Overview

   The application of a theory to subject matter offers two kinds of experiences. First, there is the opportunity to confront new material from a perspective that has proven valid to others; in this way the new material will not seem overwhelming. Second, there is the opportunity to see old material in new patterns so that valuable information is highlighted, and does not remain undiscovered. Your experience with a project in history, with gathering sources, analyzing them, fitting them to the theory, and writing about the sources to recreate an event or to understand an event, drew on all the skills we have practiced in this text. You should be ready to apply this approach to other academic subjects in the future.

CHAPTER VIII - REVISION AND WRITING
TO THE NONPROFESSIONAL AUDIENCE

"Rewriting? That means checking the spelling and punctuation and things like that."

"I usually do rewriting as I go along. I stop and check every few sentences."

"Rewriting? I never have time for it."

Every time I have asked my classes about the activity that goes on between the drafts of a paper, I have received the above responses. There are some students who suggest their rewriting might include other activities, such as adding fancy words or making the sentences flow, but for the most part rewriting to these students means edging one's way towards correctness.

I wonder how many of these students realize that for the rewriting tasks they have selected, they could get a computer to do them (perhaps someday a robot), or they could probably work a deal with the English major down the hall? Anybody well equipped with a few rules of grammar and spelling would suit their needs.

For professionals and academic researchers, on the other hand, the only people who can rewrite their papers are themselves. This is true because the tasks they attend to as rewriting have little to do with correctness and everything to do with communication. The professionals are concerned that the message of the paper is received clearly by the readers. They are aware that anything--an interruption, a bad day, poorly chosen language--can interfere with that message. As a result they turn their attention to adjusting the word choice, the sentencing, the structure, and other elements of writing, to make sure that each plays a role in communicating the message.

In order to help us differentiate between what the professional means by rewriting and what the beginner often means, let us use different terms. For rewriting tasks that are concerned with correctness, let us use the term editing. Let that mean the activities of checking for correct spelling and punctuation, and changing sentence structure for grammatical reasons. For rewriting tasks that are concerned with communication and style, let us use the term revision. Let revision mean the activities of choosing: choosing a paper structure that suits our purpose; choosing language that sets the correct tone; choosing sentence patterns that help elaborate our ideas; choosing a style that best represents us in relation to our subject and audience.

Academic Writers and Revision

Many students may not believe that academicians (as opposed to creative writers) are actually concerned with matters of revision rather than correctness, especially if the academician is a scientist. On the other hand, in my discussions with researchers across the campus I have found that in every discipline the professional researcher is concerned with effectiveness of writing, and assumes that, of course, the finished product will be correct. This is no less true for scientists and social scientists than for professors of literature. In one discussion a sociologist explained to me that if a sociologist wished to be published, he/she would have to master the writing style of the journal chosen. James Watson, in *The Double Helix,* his book describing DNA research, explains that he admired the writing style of Linus Pauling, and consciously sought to imitate it when writing up his own research. In a lecture delivered to writing students, a zoologist explained that the difficulty of good science writing was the stylistic challenge of using as few words as possible while remaining accurate and clear. Each one of these professionals is acutely concerned with the way the research is written and revised.

In their statements each of these researchers' was aware of the conditions that come together to dictate appropriate style. Each was aware that the field brings with it certain stylistic boundaries. We have already explored how the objective methods of science have required a particular paper structure and the subjective methods of literature have allowed for another structure. The sociologist was particularly aware that the journals of the field serve very strongly to reinforce the stylistic conventions common to his field. The zoologist, too, conceived of style that was appropriate to good science.

Another condition which helps each writer to shape the writing is the audience. The zoologist explained that his first audience for his research is always his fellow professionals. He explained that there is tacit agreement among colleagues that progress in research is always published first in professional publications. When writing for this audience, he can make certain assumptions. They share a world of interests, activity, knowledge and vocabulary. These readers want to know his hypothesis, methods and data, quickly and accurately. We can easily understand how this audience helps him to choose the content, the language and the style of what is written. This same zoologist has found that there are other audiences also interested in his research. There is a circle of nonprofessionals, some are hobbyists, who have wide knowledge but do not do research. They, too, want to be kept informed and are interested in his methodology, but not in order to reproduce the procedure. They, perhaps, wish to "see" him at work in a descriptive sense, they appreciate some of the technical aspects of his methods and findings, and they have an enthusiast's interest in the subject. The language used to write to this audience may be personal, appealing to the senses, and colorful. The structure of the paper might be narrative. The content, however, may not be very different from the report to the professionals. When this same scientists turns to an audience not so intimate with the details of his work, the content as well as the style may take a new turn. If his audience becomes a panel of private sponsors who might give money to support his research, then some of the content must explain the significance of his research and a good deal must explain the costs involved; if the audience is a group reviewing research at the university, then the content and style will take new turns and tone. In each case the scientist-as-writer uses all the elements of composition to make sure the audience gets the message.

When this zoologist discusses what he does with his writing when he addresses different audiences, it becomes clear that audience is one of the most important aspects in determining an appropriate style. For this zoologist, there is no such thing as a general audience. Each group of people he writes to, and he delights in writing for many different publications, each requires a special approach, a special presentation of his content, of his language, of his style. He is delighted to discuss at length just what he does to reach his audience. He explains how the opening has to "hook" the reader, he explains his word choice, and the kind of information each reader needs. He has succinct ways of characterizing each reader and he knows their responses. He knows how to adjust his style.

If we, too, would look around at the places writing is published, and the places we publish our writing, we would agree there is no entity called a "general audience." Each magazine and newspaper on our news stands is published for a particular audience, for Rhode Islanders, for hobbyists, for housewives, for decorators, for people on diets, for 7 to 10 year olds. Most of what we write is also for special audiences, our professors, our boy friends, girl friends, mothers, fathers, future employers, senators, and so on. Even though you are not professional you probably do not write to your mother the same way you write to your friend or professor. If you write to your professor to protest a failing grade, it would not be in the same words or voice or content as the same story is written to your mother and to your intimate friend. Consciously or not, your style changes.

Exercises
1. Make a list of magazines on a store shelf. For each one, identify its audience and explain how you know this identity.
2. Select one of your previous papers. What non-academic audiences might be interested in the subject? What magazine might accept an article on that subject rewritten for its audience? What would have to be changed?

Thoughts on Style and the Writing Process

"Style" has an elusive meaning. Books on style might cover any aspect of writing, from documentation to word choice. In this text, style refers to the words, the sentencing, the voice, the structure and the rhetorical approach (among other elements) any writer *chooses* to use. The word "chooses" in this context is important. Most beginning writers do not choose to write in any particular way, and in some situations, such as the hypothetical one of the failing grade, the choices happen unconsciously. But more experienced and professional writers control their writing by taking time to make these choices consciously, and by taking time to control their style. The zoologist deliberately takes much time to consider his style when he writes.

In fact, time may be the central problem for us as beginners and as busy students. We often do not seem to have the time to add to the writing process, especially if the paper is being banged out the night before its due. If, however, we reconsider the way in which many students write a paper, we may find some time we can reassign to style.

Linda Flower has spent a lot of time observing the steps students take when writing a paper. She found that one of the most common approaches of a student writer is what she calls the "perfect draft." First, the student cannot get started until a sentence is found that summarizes the main idea or exact point of the essay. Then the rest of the paper starts to flow. In reality, however, the flow lasts only for a few sentences or for a short passage. Then the student stops to reword a sentence, perhaps to scratch out a passage and start off again, only to stop soon again to rewrite. When asked what was involved in the rewrite, the student often explained that the sentence was being rewritten to sound good. When the essay is finished the only rewriting is what we have labeled as editing.

This process may sound efficient and short. In reality Linda Flower found it laden with problems, and not very efficient or leading to good papers. First of all, the time involved in finding the perfect opening sentence was inordinately long and often very discouraging to the student. It often meant writing and scratching out and tearing up papers, until the level of frustration interfered with continuing with the essay; the writing was often postponed. Second, because the first sentence became so important, the rest of the paper became close-ended; if a new idea is discovered while writing (which is not unusual), it either has to be discarded, or worked in where it would not logically fit, or the opening sentence would have to be revised, thus rendering as wasted much of the time invested in the "perfect" first sentence. Third, the start and stop method of the rest of the paper was particularly ineffective. If the student stopped to polish up the language of a sentence, searching for the right words, it often meant that the train of thought of the passage might be lost. Then the student would have to reconsider, go back a little further, and start forward with the idea once again. It was not unusual for the momentum to be simply lost, and the passage to be brought to a quick close. Sometimes the student would proceed merely from the polished sentence, possibly letting the train of thought take an unexpected twist, thus rendering the overall passage ineffective. In either case the paper would not be the "perfect" draft originally envisioned by the writer. Only if there was time to revise would the draft improve. So revision time would be needed anyway.

Linda Flower also found that much more successful essays came from a different process, multiple drafts. If the first draft did not have to be perfect, then the writing could begin much more quickly, even with an imperfect sentence or with notes and jottings. If the point of the first draft was simply to explore the ideas and the writing, the first draft went quickly and many more ideas surfaced. She also found that if genuine revision activities were taken up after the first draft, the later versions were also quickly written and much more coherent. Overall she found that multiple drafts saved time with better results.

Luckily for us, we can follow Linda Flower's research and suggestions quite easily. Much of the process we are required to follow in our projects in this text acquaints us with our content long before we sit down to write a final version. The methodology and purpose of our project help us to narrow our scope and choose a paper structure. The note taking itself presents us with usable first draft material. Nevertheless, if we take the advice of the zoologist, there is still a good deal of revision for style that must occur for a worthy final draft to be written. If we listen to Linda Flower, the most efficient time to attend to revision, to those tasks of choosing words, sentences, tone, etc. to reach out to the audience, is after the first draft. Then we can tinker with the text, play with the language, dabble in a thesaurus, polish the prose. We can take time to perfect our style.

Exercises
1. Select and peruse one magazine. Choose an article, an advertisement and an editorial, and examine every aspect of the writing, the graphics and the lay out to see how the magazine appeals to its audience.
2. Write a journal entry which describes how you must change the aspects of your writing in your original paper to be suitable for the magazine and its audience.

A Writing Project

In order to practice some of the ideas discussed by these professionals, let us take that background information and one of your papers (or several of your papers, if they concern the same subject), and revise the information for a dramatically different audience than the academic audience of the original. Choose a group, find a magazine that might be addressed to that group specifically, and write an article that might be submitted for publication. Since you are now knowledgeable in the area, and have written one paper for starters, you will be able to spend time considering revision and style. The Application section should help you take some of the important steps in the process.

Application

The discussion leading up to the assignment pointed to many tasks that are involved in this paper. First, we must find a means of analyzing audience that will help shape the paper. Second, we will review a structure that should be helpful as you write this paper. Third, we will review some of the choices you might consider as you revise.

Audience Analysis

Keeping in mind the comment that there is no such entity as a general audience for an effective writer, you should probably move as quickly as possible to select and characterize your reader. Each reader, or group of readers, can be known much as we come to know any of our acquaintances. Give the reader a name, even within a category, such as college instructor, bird watcher, house wife. Determine other obvious characteristics, such as age, educational level, social or economic brackets, important social, political or other values and attitudes, and life styles or interest. Once you have this portrait in mind, you might select the publication chosen for this assignment and browse through it to see how the editors, writers and advertisers have appealed to the reader you have portrayed. Try to notice the details of the format, the advertising, and the writing which reach out to the audience.

A second phase of this audience analysis is to use this information to determine the reader's relation to your subject. You should be able to decide the depth of the reader's knowledge of the subject, especially in relation to your knowledge of the subject. To gage this you should probably create categories of subject knowledge, such as background, significance, current developments, methods, data, interpretive skills, and future developments, and fill in the details of your audience's knowledge and your knowledge. You should also be just as thorough in gaging the reader's interest and attitude towards the subject, again in comparison with your own position. Again, find the categories that will suit your needs, such as interest level of an expert, hobbyist, novice, etc., attitude favorable, curious, ready for action, etc. When you have completed your analysis, you should have a strong sense of who your reader is and what decisions you can make as a writer.

Exercise
1. Fill in the chart at the end of this text entitled, "Chapter VIII: Audience-- Subject Analysis."

Writing the Paper

Focus and Structure
Bringing together your analysis of the publication and the reader should show you what would be appropriate subject matter, what focus or emphasis or purpose to choose, what style to aim at, and how you wish to appear to the reader. If, for example, you determine that your audience knows the subject well, is ready to take some action in relation to the subject and is well educated, you might choose to write a sophisticated analysis of one small aspect of your subject, even call for some action or suggest a direction for your reader, and you might appear to the reader as a fellow activist. On the other hand if the reader knows nothing of the subject, then you might decide to explain the significance of the subject, fill in broad background, focus in on issues that might immediately effect the reader, and appear as a concerned expert. Whatever your analysis yields, your options as a writer should be very clear and specific.

Once you have determined the special niche you wish to fill with the paper and how to reach the audience, you should be able to decide on the structure of the paper. Katula, Martin and Schwegler, in their text *Communication,* have developed a useful structural outline for a stock issues informative report that you may adapt, based on the needs of your audience. They suggest that the sections to be included are:

Background--any historical, narrative or descriptive information that will allow the audience to understand and focus in on your specific subject.

Significance--any information (descriptive, narrative, statistical, etc.,) that will draw the audience into understanding the importance or urgency of the subject.

Features--any information that explains the parts of the subject so that the audience may visualize, understand or interpret the subject, as you choose.

Good and Bad--any information that makes clear the interpretive or qualitative aspects of the subject, acknowledging the advantages/disadvantages, the problems/solutions, etc.

Procedures--any information which lays out a pattern for the audience to follow, in order to understand, or assume an attitude or take action.

Applications--any information which will guide the reader to apply the information in the essay.

This brief overview should be enough to suggest a pattern for you to follow and adjust as your audience analysis dictates. If your audience has a background in the subject, you need only focus on the subject and use key words to remind the audience of the shared background information; if your audience will not be applying the information of the report, then there is no need for the Applications section, and so on. Similarly, this brief outline, if tied in with your audience analysis, should help you decide which will be the longest section of the report, and therefore which may require much more elaborate detailing.

Even within this outline there are other rhetorical decisions to be made. How, for example, will you explain the significance of your subject? It is never enough to say to your audience, "This is important." You will not only have to find the slant which will make the subject seem important to the audience, but you will have to relate it in such a way that it sounds important. Statistics about the number of peregrine falcons left along the Taiga River in Alaska may leave cold an audience from Miami Beach, unless, perhaps, they see the issue from the perspective of pesticides entering the food chain, theirs and the birds . Even then, you might choose to present the significance in terms of numbers, or a narrative, or a description of the birds or the food chain, or another approach. The strategic choices at any point within the stock issues informative report may be:

Narration and Description--either telling a story or using sensual language to evoke the first hand experience of the subject. This tends to be colorful, subjective writing.

Analysis--taking one item or one aspect of your subject and examining the pieces or parts of the one item to understand the whole.

Comparison--taking two items to draw out similarities or differences. This helps to improve understanding of either item or both.

Classification & Division--taking groups of items and creating categories to establish order and insight.

Definition--this often clarifies the meaning of a term to make that term unique or place it in its proper perspective or clarify its current or connotative uses.

This incredibly brief summary cannot possibly pretend to cover the rhetorical choices and advantages involved in writing, but it should serve to remind you that you can control your writing by deciding how best to get to your audience and reaching for an appropriate rhetorical mode. It is often true that if a portion of your paper does not seem to be working, you might try shifting to another mode that will allow for more explanation or development, or that will allow for more or less of a personal voice. Your writing instructor, in this case, is the professional who can give the most help in making rhetorical choices. An effective way to evaluate the rhetorical effectiveness of the paper is to make the sort of double outline described and practiced in the opening chapters of this text.

Exercises

1. List the informative areas you intend to write up for your paper, and write one to two sentence summaries of the content for each area.
2. For each informative area listed in #1, select a tentative rhetorical mode which might help develop the content. Consider the following:
   a. How will you "hook" your audience (the opening)?
   b. How will you maintain the audience's interest (the body)?
   c. How will you present yourself (opening and body)?
   d. How will you create a final impact (the closing)?
3. Write a complete draft of your paper.

Choosing to Write with Style

Drawing our third lesson from the first half of this chapter, we might remind ourselves, again, that through revision we are really seeking to make choices with the elements of writing--words, sentences, and paragraphs--that will best reach our audience. If we have left time for this phase, the choices may be as creative and exciting as any other part of the writing process.

In terms of word choice, professional writers explain that they love to linger among the connotations of words, enjoying the differences, for example, between "fat," "stout," and "obese." Which one is exactly right for the subject? For the audience to see the subject? Even if colorful language seems out of place in your report, it is your responsibility to try to find the most precise word, to avoid jargon, to establish the right level of formality, and to avoid sexist language. Donald Hall, in his text *Writing Well*, advises writers to look at the types of words to make the best choices. He advises, for example, that when possible verbs be active, and that replacing forms of "to be" and "to have" with active verbs immediately improves the impact of the writing. In addition, he suggests that nouns be as specific as possible for their context; that adjectives and adverbs might easily be minimized, as well as scrutinized, for their cliche value. For in depth guidelines, I suggest you take a look at his text.

In addition, a few other quick guidelines can immediately spruce up your text. First, pronouns. Choose one and stick with it. The pronoun "I" is not as often inappropriate as many of us have been made to feel by uninformed writing teachers. If you choose another, remember to use it consistently, and not to slip into the generalized "you" unless *you* really mean the individual reader of your essay. Second, the paper will gain in immediacy if you replace generalized nouns, such as "people," with specific nouns, such as freshmen, anglers, or punks. Third, replace every word that you chose simply to impress a reader with a word that is its clearest or simplest synonym. Often, when students are writing a report or research, they feel they must sound authoritative by using fancy or difficult words. But the easiest way to sound authoritative is to be accurate. Choose the right word for your subject and you will get to your audience.

Finally, an eye towards sentencing. Instead of worrying about whether or not you have written complete sentences, remember that here, too, you have choices, for we have plenty of variation of sentence patterns in English. Francis Christensen, a scholar and rhetorician, reminded us that sentences are created by using basic patterns with infinite additions at the beginnings, ends and in the middles of sentences. If we use these additions as opportunities to add detail and concreteness to our papers, the possibilities of sentencing open up. From this perspective we can look for sentences that are merely generalizations; should these sentences remain undeveloped, not made concrete? We can look at strings of sentences to examine what detail has been added to what sentence. Have we arranged the breaks and additions in the right places? Should they be arranged differently? Try rewriting a paragraph by moving the periods to form different sentence groups. Examine a whole paragraph for the placement of sentence breaks, and for placement of strings of detail. These two types of changes can be eye opening. Rearranging often improves the impact of the writing.

As a last test of the effectiveness of your writing it is often helpful to hear your paper read aloud. If possible, let someone else read it aloud while you listen, preferably someone who is willing to be impartial and honest. You will immediately hear how easily this reader is able to follow the content and style of the essay; and you will hear, at the same time, the well developed parts and the gaps, the strong parts of the essay and the weaker ones. You will then have the rare opportunity of getting immediate feed back from a reader. Grab it to make any changes necessary to improve your essay.

Once you have tried your hand at this paper by letting revision be the primary focus of your writing, you will be ready sooner than you think to hand over to your typist a paper that might be the best you have written. As it goes into and comes out of the typewriter you might turn your attention to proofreading. The zoologist referred to many times throughout this chapter advises that proofreading is best done for spelling by reading through the text backward, word by word. Try it from the bottom up through a page of your paper to see how each word is yanked from its context and seen individually. Sentence and punctuation correction might be approached in the same manner, backwards sentence by sentence, checking for complete and correct sentences, using a handbook when necessary. Do not hesitate to correct typing errors, even on finished copy. It is far better to submit a neatly corrected manuscript than to submit one full of typographical errors; you would be blamed for the errors, not your typist.

By completing all the steps of writing and revision in this chapter you should have written a paper aimed firmly at the nonprofessional audience. You will have reviewed the tasks of audience analysis, style and subject analysis, mastered the informative report structure, and chosen the language and sentencing of your paper. Each paper you write in the future may draw on these skills.

Exercises
1. Choose the longest paragraphs in your paper. Revise the language, the sentences and the pronouns as suggested by the discussion.
2. Look through the entire paper and revise for style.
3. Evaluate and revise the whole paper for:
   a. Unity and coherence;
   b. Choice and quality of rhetorical modes and informative tasks;
   c. Complete paragraph development;
   d. Audience appropriateness;
   e. Magazine appropriateness.
4. Proofread your paper.

BIBLIOGRAPHY

Armstrong, James. "The 'Death Wish' in 'Stopping By Woods.'" *College English* 30 (1969): 440-441.

Bazerman, Charles. *The Informed Writer: Using Sources in the Disciplines.* 2nd ed. Boston: Houghton, 1985.

Bruffee, Kenneth A. *A Short Course in Writing.* Cambridge: Winthrop, 1972.

Burhans, Clinton S. "The Complex Unity of *In Our Time.*" *Modern Fiction Studies* 14 (1968): 313-328.

Christensen, Francis and Bonniejean Christensen, eds. *Notes Towards a New Rhetoric: Nine Essays for Teachers.* 2nd ed. New York: Harper, 1978.

Fowler, H. Ramsey, et al. *The Little Brown Handbook.* 2nd ed. Boston: Little, Brown, 1983.

Gondola, Joan C. and Bruce W. Tuckman. "Psychological Mood State in 'Average' Marathon Runners." *Perceptual and Motor Skills* 55 (1982): 1295-1300.

Hall, Donald. *Writing Well.* Boston: Little, Brown, 1973.

Katula, Richard A., et al. *Communication: Writing and Speaking.* Boston: Little, Brown, 1983.

Lucas, John. *Historical Consciousness of the Remembered Past.* New York: Harper, 1968.

Maimon, Elaine P., et al. *Writing in the Arts and Sciences.* Boston: Little, Brown, 1981.

Mills, C. Wright. *The Power Elite.* New York: Oxford, 1959.

Rackham, Jeff. *From Sight to Insight: Steps in the Writing Process.* 2nd ed. New York: Holt, 1984.

Sawyer, Stephen W., "Leaders in Change: Solar Energy Owners and the Implications for Future Adoption Rates." *Technological Forecasting and Social Change.* 21 (1982): 201-211.

Shotwell, James T. ed. *Records of Civilization: Sources and Studies.* New York: Columbia, 1922.

Smith, Ronald E. and Theodore M. Sharpe. "Treatment of a School Phobia with Implosive Therapy." *Journal of Counseling and Clinical Psychology* 35 (1969) 239-243.

Teggart, Frederick J. *Theory of History.* New Haven: Yale, 1925.

Thomas, Lowell. *With Lawrence in Arabia.* New York: Century, 1924.

Tuchman, Barbara W., *Practicing History*. New York: Knopf, 1981.

Watson, James D. *The Double Helix: A Personal Account of the Discovery of DNA*. New York: Antheneum, 1968.

APPENDIX I
GUIDELINES FOR DOCUMENTATION

1. When to Document--You should acknowledge every reference to the language or idea of another made within your text. This reference might be quite formal within your text or it might be made as a minor aside. In either case use the proper footnote or reference acknowledgment. This rule holds for all borrowed information except that considered "common knowledge." Knowledge may be considered held in common if it has been referred to in three texts without footnotes. You should enter into your bibliography all readings done in the course of your research, whether referred to in your text or not.

2. Location of the footnote and footnote number--This convention differs from field to field. In many of the sciences, the only in text acknowledgment consists of a parenthetical note of author and year of study, such as (Shamoon, 1975). This note appears immediately after a reference to the author, study or idea has been stated; the parenthetical information will interrupt the flow of the sentence. The parenthetical note refers to the bibliography for the full information. In the humanities, on the other hand, some academic areas require the footnote to be indicated at the end of the sentence, after the period, above the sentence line, such as.[1] This number refers to the full footnote found either at the bottom of the page or at the end of the chapter.

3. Quotations--Direct quotations of more than four words must be inserted between quotation marks, and correctly footnoted. This rule holds even if the quoted material appears within a section or a paragraph already documented for paraphrased and summarized materials. Any direct quote which is more than four typed lines in length must be isolated from the text by narrowed margins and single spaced typing. This sort of quote is footnoted, but is not surrounded by quote marks; the indentation and single spacing is enough indication that the material is quoted.

4. Paraphrases and Summaries--All reference to the ideas and language of others must be documented. However, the material which follows a formal textual introduction to an author and/or work, and which is clearly of a summarized or paraphrased nature, may be footnoted once, at the first mention of the work or author. Your discussion should then use the author's name frequently as an in text reminder that the paraphrase is continuing. (If numbered footnoting is used, then the first note may explain that all future references to the text will be to the edition listed, and page numbers may then be cited without a footnote reference. In other notation systems, this is not necessary.) If the paraphrase continues through to a new paragraph, then the reader should be alerted that the ideas of others are still being utilized by correct textual and footnote reference. A direct quote within the paraphrase would necessitate another footnote. A reference later in your paper to the same work and/or passages may require another footnote.

5. Abbreviations found in footnotes and bibliographies, etc.--Many abbreviations are used conventionally in documentary procedures; the most common are listed below. Note that two abbreviations which were once quite common in research papers are now becoming archaic in many fields: op. cit. (opere citato)--in the work cited; and loc. cit. (loco citato)--in the place cited.

e.g.--exempli gratia, for example
ed.--edition; edited by; editor (plural--eds.)
et al, et ali--and others
fig.--figure (plural--figs.)
ibid, ibidem--in the same place
id.--idem, the same or the same person
ms.--manuscript (plural--mss.)
n.d.--no date
n.p.--no; no publisher
p.--page (plural--p.p.)
passim--here and there
sic--so, thus
trans.--translator, translated by
vol.--volume (plural--vols.)

6. Quotations, interrupted or amended--Direct quotations are to be used exactly as they appear in your source. If you wish to stop a quote mid-sentence, or if you wish to stop the flow of a quoted text and pick it up elsewhere, then you must use the ellipsis or three dots ". . ." This indicates that the quoted material continues. If you wish to change a word or insert a word in the quote for the sake of clarity, then you may do so with the use of brackets [ ] around the changed or inserted material. If you wish to add emphasis to a particular portion of the quote, you may italicize or underline that portion of the quote, but you must remember to indicate the underlining is yours and not the original author's by noting at the end of the quote: [italics mine]. If a misspelling appears in the original, you must retain this in your quote, followed by (sic), indicating the misspelling is not yours.

7. Footnoting a source within a source--If you wish to use the materials of an author's which the author of your source has quoted, you must note the original within the context of the book or article you are reading. For instance, if you were reading this book, and you found a passage originally written by Kate L. Turabian which you wished to quote in your own paper, your footnote must be within the context of this book.

Kate L. Turabian, *A Manual for Writers of Term Papers, Theses and Dissertations,* 4th ed. (Chicago: University of Chicago Press, 1973), p. 82, quoted in Linda K. Shamoon, *Think/Write A Guide to Research Papers Across the Curriculum* (Iowa: Kendall-Hunt, 1985). p. 134.

8. Other uses for footnotes--Occasionally you may want to make a brief comment which has little or no direct bearing on your text; you may relegate this information to a footnote. You might also want to refer the reader to another part of your paper; this, too, may be cited in a footnote. These footnotes are called substantive or content footnotes. They are written in the proper place for footnotes and numbered accordingly; however, they use full and complete sentence forms rather than abbreviations.

Chapter I: Concepts and Definitions

A Descriptive Outline of a Laboratory Paper

I.

    A.

    B.

    C.

    D.

II.

III.

IV.

V.

    A.

    B.

    C.

VI.

Chapter II: Subject–Method–Hypothesis Analysis

General Topic Methods	Relevant Academic Hypothesis	Limitations of	Tentative Area
Sports			
Clothing			
Anorexia			
Shopping Malls			
Hemingway			

Chapter II: From Personal Interests to Hypothesis

Fill in the chart below. Make three sets of entries.

My Experience or Personal Knowledge	Related interest or issue	Generalization	Hypothesis

Your Subject	Method in detail	Narrow Focus	Data Possibly Gathered	Best Hypothesis
	Interviews:			
	Questionnaires:			
	Observations:			
	Case Study:			

Chapter VII: A Chart which Summarizes
Three Theories and their Applications

Name of
Theory

Summary of Principles

Appropriate
Application

Chapter VII: A Subject Analysis Chart
to Begin a History Project

General Subject   Questions   Sources

                                   People:

                                   Scene:

                                   Times:

                                   Sequence:

Narrow Focus:

Chapter VIII: Audience--Subject Analysis

My Knowledge	Audience's Knowledge

**Background
of Subject**

Significance

Features

**Attitudes
toward Subject**

Unknown Areas